Channel Innovation in Financial Services

A Practitioner's Guide to Development and Integration

By Sandy Vaci

Book 2 in the Keys to Sales Success series

Searching finance

First published 2011 by Searching Finance Ltd, 8 Whitehall Road, London W7 2JE, UK

ISBN: 978-1-907720-11-6

Typeset by Deirdré Gyenes

Cover image by iStockphoto

Channel Innovation in Financial Services

A Practitioner's Guide to Development and Integration

By Sandy Vaci

Book 2 in the Keys to Sales Success series

Searching finance

About the author

Sandy Vaci is an international bank executive with 30 years' experience across four continents, in close to 50 countries. He has held executive positions at companies such as Citibank's Global Consumer Bank, Procter & Gamble, the Royal Bank of Scotland Group, Raiffeisen International and the Canadian Imperial Bank of Commerce.

He is currently Senior Lecturer in Marketing and Sales at the Maastricht School of Management and the Business School of Central European University. He is also Chairman of the Supervisory Board of the Credit Bank of Moscow and advises a wide range of companies on global best practices. His client list includes Barclays Bank, UniCredit Group, Eureko Insurance, Unilever, and the National Commercial Bank of Jamaica.

As a true 'global citizen', Sandy has three home bases (Toronto, Vienna, Budapest) which he shares with his wife of 25 years, Judit. His most recent book, 'Sales and Sales Management in Financial Services: A Hands-on Guide to Global Best Practices' was also published in 2010 by Searching Finance.

Acknowledgements

The author wishes to thank the following people for their support:

Robert Zanescu, public relations, communication, corporate affairs and social responsibility director, Bancpost (Romania). For contributing the Volksbank Romania case study.

Ariana Heemi, public relations, Bendigo and Adelaide Bank (Australia). For kind permission to quote their material on community banking.

Dr Judit Acs, partner, 3-i Inc. Strategic Consultancy (Canada). For her help, support and quality control of the work.

About Searching Finance Ltd

Searching Finance Ltd is a dynamic new voice in knowledge provision for the financial services and related professional sectors. Our mission is to provide expert, highly relevant and actionable information and analysis, written by professionals, for professionals. For more information, please visit www.searchingfinance.com

Also available from Searching Finance Ltd

There are two companion volumes in the 'Keys to Sales Success' series for financial sales practitioners. Book 1, 'Sales and Sales Management in Financial Services: A Hands-on Guide to Global Best Practices' looks at branch set-ups and sales management, including needs-based selling, the implementation of best practices and moving cross-border. Book 3, 'Segmentation and Marketing in Financial Services: Best Practices from CRM to FMCG' examines current marketing practices and how they support the sales process.

CONTENTS

LIST OF TABLES AND FIGURES

Abbreviations

AC	Acquisition Cost – direct cost of acquiring a new customer or account
ACCT	Account – such as deposit, current, revolving credit accounts
ATM	Automated Teller Machine, sometimes also called ABM (Automated Banking Machine)
ATL	Above The Line marketing, e.g. advertising, PR, sponsorships, internet
BAU	Business As Usual – the level of (new) business that should be expected without proactive actions or extenuating factors (sometimes also called 'walk-in', in the case of branches)
BDR	Business Development Representative
BEP	Branch Efficiency Project
BTL	Below The Line marketing, e.g. direct mail and outbound sales calls
C/A	Current Account / Checking Account – transactional, 'household' account
CAPEX	Capital Expenditures – upfront spending for capital goods acquisition or improvements (e.g. when setting up a branch)
CC	Credit Card
CIR	Cost-to-Income-Ratio
CRM	Customer Relationship Management (sometimes, but *not* in this study, also referring to Credit Risk Management)
DIY	Do-It-Yourself, home renovation retail stores
FTE	Full Time Equivalent person – one additional headcount, assuming full time work by it, at 100%
FTL	Fixed Term Loan
GDP	Gross Domestic Product – the total local output of a country's economy
HNWI	High Net Worth Individual(s) – people with potential or worth above core customers but below private banking prospects or clients
IT	Information Technology – refers both to the department that handles software / hardware support and to the software / hardware set up itself
IVR	Interactive Voice Response system – automated call response software, usually used in call centres
JV	Joint Venture – a company set up by two or more separate entities owing it, setting direction, benefiting from gains and bearing losses together

KPI	Key Performance Indicators – essential measures to track how the business is doing on an ongoing basis
L/C	Line of Credit – revolving line, can be drawn on at will
M&A	Mergers and Acquisitions – usually refers to acquiring another business, not to being acquired
NIM	Net Interest Margin – the (average) difference between the interest rate paid on deposits and the rate charged on loans; the margin a bank makes
NPV	Net Present Value – the aggregated current value of something that may take a long time to generate returns (it accounts for the cost of the money, so current returns are more highly valued that returns later on)
NSF	No Sufficient Funds – when there are not enough funds in an account to cover payments initiated from that account by the customer
O/D	Overdraft – a line of credit attached to an account, usually a current account
PI	Private Individual segment within retail banking customers (the other main segment being SME)
P&L	Profit and Loss (responsibility) – bottom line (accountability)
POS	Point-of-Sale, for banks it also refers to 'sales finance' or 'consumer finance' – granting credit to customers at retail outlets to allow purchase of goods (or, rarely, services)
PR	Public Relations – managing a company's image with the public, without advertising or promotional means
REA	Real Estate Agent
ROA	Return On Assets
ROE	Return On Equity
S/A	Savings Account
SBU	Strategic Business Unit – usually a business unit with its own objectives, authorities and P/L responsibility
SFA	Sales Force Automation (software) – part of a CRM set up
SLA	Service Level Agreement – pre-agreed level of service deliverables between departments or units of the same company
SME	Small and Medium-sized Enterprise – small businesses
SMS	Short Messaging System – sending text messages through mobile phones
SW	Software
SWOT	Strengths, Weaknesses, Opportunities and Threats – a way to evaluate a business based on internal and external factors
TD	Term Deposit, also called Certificate of Deposit (CD), Guaranteed Investment Certificate (GIC), etc.

TOC Take on Cost – the cost of acquiring a new account, expressing the acquisition cost as a percentage of the average balance acquired with the account. Useful for fixed term, fixed balance sales, such as personal loans or fixed term deposits

TQM Total Quality Management – service quality initiatives that cover the whole company

T/L Term Loan, to be repaid over a set period of time, in instalments

U&A Usage and Attitude study – research to understand how consumers use products and how they relate to them (what expectations they have)

USP Unique Selling Proposition – the kind of benefits and features that make our offer uniquely better (different) from the competition's

VIP Very Important Person – high value customer or prospect, also referred to as 'Premium Segment'

Introduction

Why this book?

How do I set up a sales agent network? How will I control it? How much time will it take to build? How should I layer functionalities across different electronic channels? How to design the best contract for brokers and alliance partners? Are there any templates I can trust to evaluate potential branch locations? What to ask for in terms of customer relationship management (CRM) to best integrate my sales channels? How should my service quality benchmarks change across channels? What works, and what does not, in 'social media' channels? What could be the next big thing in internet banking? What is 'community banking' and how can I use it to build my network?

If you ever asked yourself questions like these, this book is for you.

How is it different?

The idea behind the book is to give you, the reader, a practical guide through the many different channel possibilities that exist today in financial services. The focus is on the practical: with examples, implementation templates, case studies, 'to dos' and 'watch outs'. Practical also means looking at frequently neglected channels such as intermediaries, sales agents, branch agents and alliance deals. While social media is more fashionable these days, third-party channels are still a good bet for an immediate, practical way to boost scale and flexibility, and to cut costs.

What does it have?

We start with the basics of branches: location selection and layouts. Next comes outsourcing to local entrepreneurs, via branch agents or franchises. Independent sales agents and building and managing third-party relationships are also discussed. We also examine remote electronic delivery: internet, phone, mobile, kiosks, ATMs, even 'virtual banking' and social media channels.

How will it help me?

By the time you finish this book, you should feel comfortable evaluating, recommending and starting to build any of the channel options reviewed. You will know what to expect, what to watch out for, how to cover the downside and how best maximise the potential. And, hopefully, you will have a few creative ideas of your own, using the examples from the book and developing them in different ways. And if you are not a practitioner yourself, then you will learn how to help those who build your channels and what to expect from them in return.

Above all, I hope this book makes clear what I believe in:

- Real people, consumers, customers, come first. Whatever the channel, however futuristic it looks, we should constantly focus on how we can best serve the people to whom we owe our profit: our customers. It follows that 'real world rules' apply – if we can address real needs better than the competition, we will win. Let them get drawn into technology. Let us get immersed in customer focus.
- It makes sense to own the customer relationship, rather than the channel that links us. Channels cost money, relationships make money. The main challenge is to control my distribution (what and how it delivers, for how

much money) without actually owning it. The next challenge is to integrate new developments into what I already have, rather than throwing away what I have built so far.

I hope you will enjoy and benefit from this survey of channel innovation. If you have any comments, please contact either the publisher at enquiries@searchingfinance.com or me directly at sandyvaci@yahoo.com.

You can also contact me at the above e-mail address if you need more in-depth help or support. That is what I do now. I help companies become the best, by helping them integrate global best practices into what they have – instead of advocating throwing away your current practices so that I can sell you something new...

If you feel there are things missing on sales basics, sales processes through the different channels and sales management practices, I have a suggestion: why not check out my other book, 'Sales and Sales Management in Financial Services: A Hands-on Guide to Global Best Practices', also published by Searching Finance. It deals with the many components of sales and gives examples of global best practices in each area. It is the perfect companion guide to this review on channels.

This book is actually Book 2 in a three-volume series entitled 'Keys to Sales Success'. The first two books will soon be followed by a third, 'Segmentation and Marketing in Financial Services – Best Practices from CRM to FMCG'. It will review the latest marketing practices and how they support the sales process. Together, these books form a complete hands-on guidance package for sales professionals.

Happy reading!

Chapter 1
Branches – the basics

Industry experience over recent years shows that branches are here to stay, in more or less the same format as they are today. Market research also tells us that branches are still the most used of all delivery channels. It is therefore imperative, before considering other channels, that we examine the most channel-relevant issues of branches: location selection and layout design.

This is all the more important, first because branches are a cornerstone of multi-channel bank set-ups, and second, location and layout selections are also important for new 'branch derivative' channels such as branch agents and kiosks.

Therefore we review first all the above elements and present templates for their application.

Location selection

The two major questions any branch location selection approach must answer are:

1. Should we open / keep a branch in this general area?
2. If yes, where should we locate it?

The first can be answered based on macro criteria – general guidelines; the second, based on micro criteria – local guidelines.

Location selection at both levels should be scorecard driven to ensure consistency. Scorecard criteria must be agreed upfront and should not be deviated from. Agreed elements of scorecards should include:

1. Types of criteria used;
2. How to assign score values for each criterion;
3. Weighting of score values to derive composite value;
4. Decisions driven by composite values (cut-off points).

Macro criteria

Macro criteria should include:

- Market potential –
    - Population base;
    - Catchment potential;
    - Size of target segment(s);
    - Value of prospect base per capita;
    - Income per capita (if 'value per capita' not available);
    - Current market share, other own branches in area;
- Competitive environment –
    - Presence of competition, scored on an 'opportunity / threat' scale;
- Internal financial feasibility –

- Revenue expectations per staff (e.g. discounted cashflow needed);
- Cost projected per staff (e.g. CAPEX needed).

Micro criteria

Micro criteria normally include:

- Security;
- Accessibility;
- Visibility;
- Traffic – volume and type, variability (seasonal, daily);
- Mass transit presence;
- Parking;
- Site size, availability and flexibility;
- Local development expectations;
- Contract issues, cost.

Macro scorecard

Each of the eight sub-components of the three major elements should have the following defined for it:

- Calculation / definition;
- Scoring criteria;
- Weighting criteria.

Note: It is either 'value of prospect base per capita' or 'income per capita', but not both, hence eight sub-categories, not the nine listed. Weighting of their values may differ, based on which one is used. If 'value per prospect' can be calculated, a higher weighting should be used than if only 'income per capita' is available.

Examples

Population base

- Defined as those living or working in town;
- Scores:
  - 1 if below 10,000;
  - 2 if 10,000 to 50,000;
  - 3 if 50,000 to 100,000;
  - 4 if 100,000 to 500,000;
  - 5 if above 500,000;
- Weight in total composite score at 20%.

Catchment potential

- Defined as the percentage of the population base that can be reached from a given location;
- Scores:
  - 1 if below 2%;
  - 2 if 2% to 5%;
  - 3 if 5% to 10%;
  - 4 if 10% to 20%;
  - 5 if above 20%;
- Weight in total composite score at 10%.

Size of target segment

- Defined as the percentage of the catchment potential base that falls within the bank's target for new customers;
- Scores:
  - 1 if below 5%;
  - 2 if 5% to 15%;
  - 3 if 15% to 35%;
  - 4 if 35% to 75%;
  - 5 if above 75%.
- Weight in total composite score at 10%.

Value of prospect base per capita / income per capita

- Either the revenue that can be expected to be made on each relationship sourced from the target segment, or the average income per capita in the area;
- Scores: depend on the bank's profit model and hurdle rates;
- Weight in total composite score at 20% (if revenue figure is available) to 10% (if only income numbers are available).

Current market share

- Defined as the percentage of the target segment the bank already has in the area, through its other branches or through other channels;
- Scores:
  - 1 if over 50%;
  - 2 if 50% to 25%;
  - 3 if 25% to 10%;
  - 4 if 10% to 5%;
  - 5 if less than 5%;

- Weight in total composite score at 10%.

Competition

To assign score value for the competitive environment one should do 'sub-scoring' first, to assess if competitive presence is an opportunity or a threat. Having weak competitors in an area may be an advantage because the bank can provide a better alternative. This could mean a ready supply of customers defecting from weaker competitors. However, the opposite is true with stronger competitors.

A way to assess competitors is to look at key elements of their presence, assign values to them and weigh them. For simplicity, the assigned values could be between -5 (when they are worse than us, hence an opportunity) and +5 (when they are better and, hence, a threat). Weighting factors could be between 4 and 1, based on the importance of each area. The suggested four key elements to be used to assess whether they are an opportunity to source customers from, or a threat to lose customers to, are:

1. Service level compared to us – better, same or worse. This is the most important factor, suggested weight: 4;
2. Positioning – level of overlap between their target segment and ours, their positioning to the market and ours. Suggested weight: 3;
3. Communication strength – how effectively they communicate, how strong their media presence and share of mind is. Suggested weight: 2;
4. Size – their resources, national distribution coverage, etc. Suggested weight: 1.

The above approach would give a score value between -20 and +20 for each competitor. Multiplying the score values by the number of their branches in our trade area, then totalling up these values provides an overall score for the competitive environment. This score is usually between +100 and -100, based on five competitive branches in a given trade area. The widest practical range experienced in the market should then be split into five bands and score values assigned to them. A score of 5 should be the best for us, corresponding with the lowest competitive band. A score of 1 should correspond to the highest competitive band.

The 1 to 5 score value assigned could then be weighted at 15% for the total composite score of the scorecard.

Revenue per staff

- Appropriate internal definition (yearly gross revenue, net revenue, discounted cashflow, other);
- Scores: depend on bank's profit model and hurdle rates;
- Weight in total composite score at 10%.

Expense per staff

- Appropriate internal definition (CAPEX, yearly total allocated costs, other);
- Scores: depend on the bank's profit model and hurdle rates;
- Weight in total composite score at 5%.

Comments

1. Weighting in the total composite score can of course vary, based on each bank's objectives and strategies. However, the weightings described so far add up to about 70% for market potential, 15% for competitive factors and 15% for internal factors. This has been proven as a fairly good overall split, because market potential should be by far the most important factor in the overall decision to open or close a branch. Within the internal financial factors, it is also better to weight revenue more heavily than costs, since the latter depends more on strictly internal, controllable, factors.
2. The total composite weightings should of course add up to 100%.
3. Each location should be scored for each criterion, score values weighted and added up. The total composite score value should then drive open / close / review decisions. The maximum total weighted composite score value for the scorecard described here is 500.
4. It is acceptable to have tolerance ranges around composite score values, of about 10% in each direction, where management may decide which way to swing the decision.
5. Based on the above, for example, branch location decisions at the macro level could be as follows:
   - Total score of 300 and above – keep / open;
   - Total score of 200 to 300 – review;
   - Total score of 200 or less – close / do not open;
   - In each case a +/- 25 score difference can be overridden by management.

It is strongly suggested that the scorecard approach outlined in this section be templated in an easy to use Excel spread sheet or similar, using the logic presented. While a detailed description such as the one given here is useful, experience suggests only templated branch location scorecards are used with any frequency. It is simply too cumbersome to use manuals for this purpose.

Micro scorecard

A separate scorecard for local guidelines can also be developed. The simplest way is again to assign score values and weighting factors to each. However, local selection criteria are on the one hand more qualitative (e.g. assessing visibility) and on the other hand more cut and dried (e.g. contract and cost issues). As a result, local site selection usually has a higher level of personal input from qualified professionals and less of a 'template driven', quantitative (statistical) approach.

Premises

A lot has been written about branch layouts and design and most banks have their own 'model branch' guidelines already. This is therefore not the focus of this study. Premises will only be discussed to the extent that is essential as being an influencer of branch sales efficiency.

The following guidelines are recommended for an efficient model branch design:

- The layout must be inviting, open, easy to walk into. Walk-in traffic is an important element of building the business and should not be discouraged. Similarly, the windows should allow a view into the interior. The premises should also be lit during off hours. These are basic rules but often disregarded;
- The overall design should be high quality but in a human way. It should not look 'too expensive'. It should definitely not look too intimidating;
- The layout and signage should clearly direct customers and prospects to the right area. A (potential) customer should never be allowed to line up twice by mistake, choosing the wrong area first. Many of them would rather walk out than line up again – a loss of potential business;
- The meeter / greeter function should be part of the branch design if at all economically feasible (in mid- to larger-sized branches). The objectives of this are to speed up processing customers and to ensure that any walk-in prospect is captured efficiently;
- Areas should be clearly blocked off using different (but complementary looking) materials and internal design elements. Consideration for defining different areas include:
  - Type of transaction:
    - High speed self-service transactions using ATMs or other self-serve terminals;
    - Interactive transactions with tellers / cashiers, requiring highly efficient and convenient processes;
    - More time-demanding consultative selling / servicing interactions, such as opening more complicated accounts, discussing needs;
    - Involved discussions, for example discussing mortgage needs or investment portfolio set-ups;
  - Type of customer segment:
    - SME (small and medium-sized enterprises, 'small business') clients. They may need specially trained account managers. Their cash in/out activities can be very time consuming, requiring drop-off boxes and special processes to handle counting the money during off hours. Their upfront sales sessions can be very involved, taking a long time;
    - Premium customers. They may need a separate area for discussing their needs, with dedicated account managers;
  - Type of sales activity:
    - As discussed later in this chapter (under 'Capacity reallocation'), physical space needs to be separated out for those sales staff involved in proactive prospecting for parts of their time. A good model branch design takes this into account upfront;

- Customer needs (e.g. fast cash transactions, privacy for sales consultations) should be taken into account. Similarly, customer needs should be researched whenever fundamental decisions on the branch design are considered. One example may be whether or not to introduce a 'take a number' system. Often management will argue that such an approach denigrates the image of the bank, by bringing it closer to a post office outlet for example. However, customers tend to like the approach if handled right, because it ensures no accidental double lining up and has an element of basic fairness, 'first come, first served'. This may especially be important for elderly, and well-to-do, clients;
- Processes must be part of the model branch design. It is not enough to have a pleasant, efficient layout. Sales and administrative processes should also be 'model branch-compliant' to ensure the efficient layout is matched by efficient processes, using it to full advantage;
- 'Stick close to your knitting'. In other words, keep in mind that a bank branch, at the end of the day, should be just that – a bank branch. Not a coffee shop, not a kindergarten, not a travel agency; customers expect a branch. Studies (e.g. 'Branch of the Future', by Novametrie) show that more than three-quarters of consumers expect their ideal branch to closely resemble their current branch and not be of a radically different design.

Results to be expected

If site selection is done right, and other elements of sales management implemented properly, the goals shown in Table 1.1 should be achievable with new branches.

Table 1.1: Branch break-even and payback benchmarks

	Break-even	Payback
Private individual customers only	3 to 5 years	6 to 8 years
Mixed-branch, including SME	1 to 2 years	3 to 4 years

Source: 3-i Inc

Chapter 2

Branch agents – 'near sourcing' to local entrepreneurs

Turning existing traditional branches into independently owned and managed agent locations, or expanding the distribution network by setting up branch agent outlets (instead of traditional bank branches), is an excellent way to boost sales efficiencies. This chapter deals with this new approach to the traditional physical outlet. It reviews its definition and benefits and provides a practical 'how to' guideline to setting up and managing such a network for best results.

The 'how to' area is organised into functional headings to make navigation easier. This way the reader can look up the area where advice might be needed – and skip over details of less interest at that particular time. As with the previous chapter, the objective is to allow the reader to understand the concept fully and start preparing business / implementation plans immediately – using the specific information provided.

Definition

In short, branch agents are self-employed, independent agents who sell and service exclusively the products provided or approved by the bank, under the bank's brand. Branch agents are commission compensated, based on their portfolio growth and size, service and risk quality, and audit measures. They have an exclusive contract with the bank, which is normally time unlimited – that is, it does not require renewals but has termination clauses instead. The concept provides efficiency, flexibility and speed of implementation benefits to banks by outsourcing sales and service activities, plus personnel and investment costs to local entrepreneurs – but in a closely controlled way.

A more detailed description of branch agents is as follows:

- Independent enterprises, with an operating licence to mediate (sell and service) the financial and other services of the bank, on the bank's behalf, on an exclusive basis. 'Services of the bank' here include not only the bank's own offers, but those third-party services which the bank would offer through its other channels. These, for example, may be third-party investment funds or insurance products;
- Branch agents operate under the bank's name, on premises selected and financed by themselves but approved by the bank. They can sign on the bank's behalf and can conclude customer contracts in the bank's name – the same way as a branch manager can;
- Branch agents are independent profit centres, responsible for their own expenses and compensated by the bank through a performance-based commission system which is regularly reviewed;
- Banking products, services, access to the bank's system, procedures, rules, forms, contracts, training, know how, professional and technical support are all provided by the bank, free of charge. In addition, the bank would normally provide start-up support to new branch agents;
- Branch agents employ their own personnel, with help from the bank as required. Branch agents own their business and may sell it or pass it over to family members. However, the bank must approve the new owner before a

transfer of the enterprise can take place. If the branch agent cannot find an appropriate new owner, they can offer the agency to the bank, which will find a suitable new agent for it.

Different concepts

The branch agent concept has been in use for a number of years in many different markets with good success. However, there has also been considerable confusion between branch franchises, branch agents and franchise agents.

- Branch franchises (or franchisees) pay a franchise fee to the bank for the right of using the bank's brand, for having access to the bank's products to sell and for the support they receive from the bank.
- Branch agents do not pay a franchise fee and normally receive most of the support the bank provides to its own branches, free of charge.
- Franchise agents can be either of the above. It is best to avoid using this term to ensure clarity of definitions. Unfortunately, branch agent set-ups have often been described as franchise agents in the past, giving rise to considerable confusion.

Benefits

Branch agent set-ups provide significant benefits to banks, independent entrepreneurs (the agents), consumers and customers – but only when structured and managed right. The dual win-win objective for both the bank and the agent gives the concept a natural advantage over branch franchising. This is because the objectives of the agent and bank are better aligned, for a longer term, than that of a franchisee and a bank franchisor:

- Agents are not required to pay a franchise fee. In addition, they receive start up support from the bank. This makes it easier for them to start up the business and allows the bank a larger pool of potential applicants to choose from;
- Agent contracts are normally time unlimited, removing unnecessary renegotiations and pressures. There is also no potential for franchise fee increases – yet another issue that could create adversarial relationship between the bank and its agent or franchise partners.

Key benefits to banks

- Lower capital requirements due to reduced number of branches;
- Lower headcount because neither the agents nor their employees are employees of the bank;
- Faster start-up and better flexibility for the above two reasons;
- Better efficiencies. Branch agents, when compared to bank branches, generate about 20% higher cross-sell and 35% higher revenue. In addition to the higher cross-sell ratio, the higher revenue is also driven by stronger focus on higher margin products, to generate higher commissions. It is also due to higher

retention rates. Experience shows that branch agents deliver higher service quality than corresponding branches and, hence, are better able to retain their best customers;

- Faster break-even. Branch agents should reach break even in three years, instead of the average five-year period for comparable bank branches;
- Higher NPV (net present value). On an eight-year basis (to allow for the five years leading up to break-even for a branch) branch agent locations represent about 135% of the NPV of a comparable branch location;
- Wider geographic coverage. Because of the above dynamics branch agents can be profitable in locations, such as smaller communities, where regular bank branches are not profitable.

Benefits to agents

- Ability to build equity. The value of an agency increases as its business increases. This equity can be later sold or retained in the family;
- Control. Over their own employment, their business, their costs. For example, branch agents can usually get essentially the same goods and services as the bank at 75% or less of the bank's cost. This is partly because they are able to negotiate small-scale deals with suppliers better (it is also because some of the stringent 'model branch' regulations are relaxed for branch agents);
- Tax advantages. As independent entrepreneurs, branch agents usually enjoy tax breaks in most jurisdictions that employees do not get;
- High earning potential. It should take no more than two years for a branch agent to generate positive cashflow. After that, their earning potential can increase rapidly. Industry experience shows that a good branch agent can comfortably generate for himself net income five times higher than an equally good branch manager in a similar branch.

Consumer benefits

- Better access to quality services, especially in smaller communities;
- Higher service quality. Customer service provided by branch agents is at least as good as that provided in traditional branches and, in most cases, higher. Branch agents have a vested interest in keeping their customer base, as any portfolio erosion would immediately affect their commission. In addition, agents have a lower turnover than branch managers and are 'embedded' in the local community. This results in a better understanding of local needs. Also, a 'pride factor' acts as an incentive to provide outstanding services in their neighbourhood.

Note that it is essential that a business case be prepared not only from both the bank's and the branch agent's perspective for evaluating the viability of a branch agent set-up. It does not matter if the bank has an outstanding model, if it does not ensure an acceptable business proposition for the agent / entrepreneur. Long-term success is guaranteed only if both parties benefit.

Control

Maintaining adequate control over an outsourced set-up such as branch agents is of paramount importance to the end business owner (the bank). Audit, control and risk management are part of this and will be detailed later in this chapter. For overall business control, however, the following guidelines must be followed:

1. Certain essential elements of the branch agent set-up must be owned by the bank. These so-called 'key control items' are needed for the agent to stay in business. Owning them directly allows the bank to simply take them back in case of a serious dispute between the bank and the agent. This puts the bank in a favourable bargaining position – the agent is essentially out of business while the dispute is on.
2. To ensure positive relationship with agents, the above elements are then provided free of charge to the agents. Their direct ownership by the bank is explained as a business continuity requirement by the bank and as additional free support to make the agent successful.
3. These essential elements should include:
    - Exterior signs and bank logos;
    - Bank stationery;
    - Cash and cash dispensers (tills);
    - Self-service banking terminals on premises, if any;
    - All bank software and access lines to the bank's systems;
    - Maintenance of above items as required.
4. No more than 80–85% of the total outlets should be branch agents. The remaining 15–20% outlets must remain fully owned and controlled bank branches in central, 'node' locations. Handling individual, serious contract disputes following the action outlined in point 1 above may not work if the agents form an alliance to put undue pressure on the bank. In that case, it is essential that all customers and customer information is transferred to bank-owned and controlled branches as soon as necessary, with as little inconvenience to customers as possible. By keeping own branches in central locations, ready to receive transferred customers, the bank maintains a favourable negotiating position in case of an agent alliance to pressure the bank.

Start-up support

Overview

A start-up package to new branch agents should be provided by the bank, covering the first three years of the agent's operation. This package has dual objectives:

A) Ensuring a successful start for both the agent and the bank; and

B) Generating immediate goodwill and commitment from the new agent.

The package should cover the first three years because it should take no longer than that for a reasonably performing new agent to start generating adequate income, covering all expenses. (Break-even for the agent should be around two years, on average.) The package should also be regressive. That is, its value must decline for each new year. A good start-up package, ensuring success, should contain the following:

- Interest-free loan;
- Promotional budget;
- Rental subsidy;
- Training;
- Salary or deferred draw;
- The essential elements described under 'Control' above.

New vesus existing locations

If the branch agent outlet is created by turning an existing branch into an agent location, different rules need apply. The approach should also be different if the existing branch manager takes over, as opposed to a new agent (entrepreneur) investing in the location.

- If the existing branch manager takes over, the interest-free loan and promotional budget components should be eliminated and the rental subsidy part provided at 50% of what is described under the next heading. The rest of the package should stay as proposed.
- If an entrepreneur takes over as the new owner, the interest-free loan should be eliminated and the promotional budget, rental subsidy and salary parts of the package should be offset against the value of three years' projected commission based on the existing portfolio, plus the one-time acquisition bonus based on the current customer base. The training and essential elements parts should remain the same. However, if the existing branch location has a poor enough business to be a 'quasi new start', the rental subsidy component may even be increased, as outlined later on.

Interest-free loan

The main reason for this loan is to help the agent pay for the equipment, furnishing and decoration of the new location. A good sample loan package can be structured as follows:

- Stand-by credit facility granted by the bank, with five-year term, which can be used to pay for qualified expenses supported by invoices;
- Maximum amount of no more than 50% of cost of starting up a similar-sized bank branch (maximum can be lowered to 33% if needed for financial reasons and if there are enough qualified agent applicants with adequate finances);
- Interest rate of 0% for the first three years, preferential secured loan rate after that;

- The bank pays 100% of instalments in the first year, 66% in the second year, 33% in the third year and nothing after that.

Promotional budget

New branch agents should be encouraged to do their own promotions and business development. To help this, a yearly promotional budget, equal to the matching local marketing budget for a similar branch, should be set up. The bank should pay 100% of costs in the first year, 66% in the second year and 33% in the third year. These funds should only be used for direct marketing and direct customer acquisitions.

Rental subsidy

Once the new branch agent location is agreed with the bank, the bank could subsidise it by 75% in the first year, 50% in the second year and 25% in the third year. This is to help the new agent with initial cashflow, while keeping costs down for the bank and encouraging the agent to negotiate a low rent.

If an existing branch location is turned into a branch agent site, the rental subsidy may be granted at 100% for the first year, 66% for the second year and 33% for the third year. This is in recognition of the fact that the branch agent may not have any short-term control over rental costs which had been previously agreed by the bank.

The exception to this rule is when the branch location has significant customer and product portfolios which generate adequate income coverage for all expenses upfront, including rent or lease payments. Such situations need to be reviewed on a case-by-case basis, using the 'offset' method described above under 'New versus existing locations'.

Training

All training costs (tuition fees, materials) for approved training for both the branch agent and his/her staff should paid by the bank for the first three years. However, the cost of days lost from the business, travel and other expenses should be born by the agent.

Salary

A salary, equivalent to 75% of a starting branch manager's salary for a similar outlet, should be paid to the new agent in the first year. This should then drop to 50% equivalent in the second year and 25% in the third year. In very good, unexploited, new locations with significant business expectations this salary can be treated as a draw against commissions later.

Financial implications

While the whole starter package as described above may seem like a 'sweet deal' for a branch agent, in my experience such a package is needed to ensure fast start-up and long-term success. It should also be noted that the significant financial advantages branch agents provide to banks (higher NPV, faster break-even) have been achieved with packages up to 25% more expensive than the one described here.

The guiding philosophy is to enable the new agent to do his best and provide enough coverage to avoid early attrition. Carefully selected branch agents do not abuse the package. In fact, most new branch agents work very hard despite the financial relief provided. For example, experience shows that the average new branch agent will not take any vacation for the first three years but will put all their time into building the business.

Once again, the approach proposed here is different from the branch franchising model recommended, and practiced, by many. Branch franchising initiatives often start with a bidding process for franchise locations. They also lack the start-up support package and put the full financial burden on the entrepreneur. Finally, franchise fees are sometimes raised in line with the overall performance of the whole franchisee community. All these would lead to a significant upfront benefit to the bank, but create additional challenges to would-be franchisees. This, in turn, can easily undermine the long-term viability of such initiatives.

Location

There should be no major differences between selecting locations for branch agent outlets and traditional bank branches, as long as their offers and target segments are the same. Of course, the selection criteria must reflect the nature of the outlet. Branch agents are best suited for selling and servicing retail offers and not for corporate banking or private banking. In general, the criteria can be split into two groups:

- General criteria – market potential, competitive environment; and
- Local criteria – accessibility, visibility, traffic, parking, site size and flexibility.

Detailed branch location selection criteria are discussed in greater detail in Chapter 1.

Premises

Branch agent premises are branded under the bank's own brand. They should provide the same overall visual appearance, quality impression and customer ease as the bank's own branches. However, a number of differences exist.

Size

Branch agent locations are smaller, rarely more than 50% of the average size of the bank's own branches. Most agents would start with very limited staffing:

- Agent – as the manager, business development officer and main account manager combined;
- One teller/cashier;
- One extra account manager, if needed;

- Possibly one back-office support person, depending on the level of decentralisation at the bank.

This staffing level then drives the design and layout of the branch agent site.

Appearance

Branding and quality impressions are regulated but in most cases strict 'model branch design' requirements are relaxed, allowing use of less expensive materials. In case of significant branch agent development efforts, it is recommended that a separate 'branch agent design manual' be produced, to ensure a standardised appearance for these outlets.

Layout

In line with the smaller size, model branch layouts are usually changed for branch agent outlets. While the essential elements usually remain (self-service zone, consultation area, cashier/teller) most of them would be smaller, some of them are modified and some elements omitted altogether. The meeter / greeter function, a staple of today's model branch design, is usually eliminated, together with its place in the layout. Consultation areas may be open, instead of the usual closed section prescribed by model branch manuals. Similarly, some standard elements of back offices (such as change rooms, a separate stationery room) may be omitted. However, customer convenience and staff safety are not to be compromised.

Products

Unlike the strictly customer acquisition–oriented sales agents (see Chapter 3 for more), branch agents should be allowed to sell all retail products that traditional retail branches of the same bank would sell. Arguments for limited product range may come up, guided by either cost considerations (IT, training, risks, size, etc) or by target segment arguments (small trade area potential, limited local demand and similar). However, in my experience it is essential that branch agents be allowed to offer the full range offered by branches. This is for a number of reasons:

- Customers of branch agents are customers of the bank and should not be discriminated against with an inferior offer range, due to their branch location;
- Branch agents are branded under the bank's name and therefore must fully offer all the benefits expected from that brand;
- Restricting the product range reduces cross-sell and the general sales efficiency of the agent;
- A restricted product range inevitably leads to customer attrition;
- Branch agents must feel as part of the bank overall, even if they are in the business for themselves. They should never feel discriminated against.

Services

Contrary to the recommended full product range approach, service offers need to be somewhat restricted with branch agents. The definition of services that could be performed by them must satisfy customer service quality requirements. On the other hand, branch agents need to be restricted from poaching the customers of other agents or branches.

Generally, a branch agent should be able to provide all the services a traditional branch can provide but should not be able to transfer a customer relationship without authorisation from the outlet that currently owns that relationship.

A branch agent should be able to:

- Open a new customer relationship or new product / service / account;
- See and change customer or account information for both its own customers and for customers of other outlets;
- Accept cash and pay out cash into / from accounts;
- Accept or initiate product applications, even if he is not allowed to conclude the opening of the account (this may be the case, for example, with some loan applications or investment offers).

On the other hand, a branch agent should not be allowed to:

- Transfer an account or relationship from another outlet to his own, unless authorised by the outlet currently owning that account or relationship;
- See the product, account or customer portfolios of other outlets;
- Generate contact lists from central data sources or from information residing at other outlets.

It is recommended that branch agents are not compensated for service activities. The commission structure (detailed later) should focus on new customer acquisitions, portfolio size and quality measures. By measuring customer service quality, and tying the payment of commission to it, a good level of service is ensured even for 'not own' customers.

However, no extra funds are to be paid for providing these services. This is to keep focus on growing the business instead of inflating the volume of service activities to generate income, while producing no extra revenues. In addition to keeping focus on revenue generation, this approach also reduces commission complexity and, hence, operational costs. While this point may be hotly debated during the setting up of a branch agent network, I would strongly caution not to open up the commission structure to service activities.

IT support

As noted earlier, branch agents should not be used on their own as 100% of a physical distribution network. Therefore, when considering branch agents, one faces the IT challenge of accommodating them in addition to other channels, instead of having the luxury of simply designing a standalone system just for them.

There are three IT challenges when integrating branch agents into a standard banking system:

- One needs to be able to define access rights and allowed activities, which may be different from those allowed for other channels. Consider, for example, the types of services not allowed to be performed by branch agents, as outlined in the previous section;
- A reliable and auditable commission tracking and allocation system is needed, linking to a business tracking module;
- The added complexity of integrating a fundamentally different channel, dealing with non-bank employees, yet linked with all other channels directly owned and controlled by the bank.

Unless the bank already has a system with flexible access rights and allowed activities built in, a so-called intermediary layer to handle this function may need to be developed. This approach is recommended over changing each of the system components with which branch agents may have interaction. This approach has several benefits:

- It avoids having to change several system components, dealing individually with all IT items that branch agents may come in contact with. Therefore, it can save significant time, effort and expense;
- It allows for further integration of other channels, such as sales agents, who may also have restricted access and service rights. By setting up a central 'traffic cop' layer further integration will be much easier;
- Access rights can be changed more easily if business changes dictate it. Instead of having to change each individual IT module, changes in the intermediary layer (most likely in a simple table format) can reconfigure rights across all channels and IT modules. Note that this may be essential from a control perspective (more detail on this can be found under 'Control' above).

Commission tracking systems are available on the market. Their integration into existing set-ups should pose no major problems.

By taking the route of adding the intermediary layer governing access and service rights, the complexity of multi-channel integration is also significantly reduced.

Organisation

The key organisational challenges can be broken into five areas, corresponding to the following questions:

1. How to stage the introduction of the new set-up into the organisation? How many steps to use to lead up to the desired end state?
2. At which level should one introduce the agent concept? District manager? Branch manager? Below branch manager?
3. How to integrate branch agents into the sales / distribution area? What should the reporting lines be?

4. How to provide support to branch agents? In the traditional areas (such as marketing, IT, etc)? In any new areas that may need to be defined (for example special 'agent advisers' or similar)?

5. Who to recruit as agents to guarantee success? How to handle the process internally and externally?

Staging the introduction

Adding new locations as branch agents is naturally a one-step process. Turning existing branch locations into agent outlets may either be a one-step or a two-step process, depending on the readiness of the sales organisation. If individual (or at least branch-level) target setting, tracking and rewards are not in place, these should be introduced before moving towards converting branches into agent outlets. Otherwise, the organisation is simply not ready to understand the concept.

However, it should also be noted that the so-called 'shadow agent' set-up is not needed as an extra step. This stage is advocated by some practitioners, as a 'concept with training wheels' interim stage. The idea is to get the organisation ready to think entrepreneurially and to define the value of existing branch locations better. This is to be accomplished by introducing a profit-sharing concept with branches and by forcing internal competition. At the end of a set time period results are evaluated and new, higher values can be attached to branches (compared to their value under the standard branch management system). This value can then be used to set the franchise price for the outlet.

Because the branch agent concept is different from the branch franchise approach, the internal valuation provided by this method is not needed. The value of an agent location can be more simply estimated by the 'three years' commission' rule detailed earlier in 'New versus existing locations.

Organisational level of agents

The natural organisational unit for an agent is at the branch level, as opposed to below or above. It follows then that branch agents should operate at the equivalent of branch manager level.

Independent roles defined below the branch level are sales agents, described in more detail in Chapter 3. They are usually linked to branches or branch agents and have a narrower, acquisition-only focus.

There are examples of turning district manager roles into independent entrepreneurs. Sometimes this higher level of 'franchising' is justified by lack of enough high-quality internal talent at the branch manager level. There are several reasons why this should be avoided:

- If talent availability is an issue internally, then external talent will be needed in any case. Raising the level at which 'entrepreneurial outsourcing' is introduced will not solve the issue. The new district manager-level agent will be saddled with inferior branch managers, making it doubly difficult for him to dynamically improve business performance;

- By starting at the branch level, initial investment for would-be agents is lower. This, in turn, attracts a wider range of talent from which to choose;
- It is preferable to build from the bottom up than in reverse. Branch agents have the upside potential of opening new outlets, and developing a 'district of agents' if their performance justifies it. This provides added incentive for them to perform.

Integration and reporting

Having defined agents at the branch level, the key question is whether to roll branch agents up as a group, or mix agents and traditional branches within each sales district. The preferred way is to mix branch agents and branch managers within districts, with the same district manager being responsible for both branches and agents within a given area. This approach accomplishes the following:

- It integrates branch agents into the fabric of the organisation better, allowing them to feel being part of the bank (while maintaining their independence) and learning from others, including branch managers;
- It provides an ongoing aspiration to branch managers, by letting them directly observe the dynamic agent culture;
- It allows district managers to grow, forcing them to manage not only employees but also independent agents – a valuable skill for career progression;
- It makes it more difficult for agents to form a common front against the bank (see point 4 under 'Control' above);
- It makes it easier to track and control the branch agent network, by using uniform procedures across branches and agents at the lowest possible control level (the level of individual outlets).

Support functions

Several of the support areas have already been reviewed. For example:

- Training – provided free of charge, upfront training mandatory;
- IT – provided free of charge as an 'essential element';
- Sales – district manager to provide;
- Marketing – central support is free (for example, no franchise fee to pay for brand advertising), local marketing paid for by the branch agent, with central budget support for the first three years after opening a new outlet.

Given the significant differences between branches and agents, additional support (involving extra FTE headcount) should be planned for. Three key positions are recommended:

- Branch agent manager – an overall functional expert, with responsibility for the efficient development and management of the branch agent network, supporting the district managers;

- Control and audit manager – responsible for ongoing control and management of the commission system;
- Co-ordinator – helping ensure smooth ongoing operation of the network on a daily basis, liaising with agents, plus with marketing, HR, IT and other departments to facilitate support to branch agents as needed

The above three positions should reside within the Sales area of the organisation.

Some organisations also set up a 'buddy system' between agents and branch managers. This can be useful to help new agents and promote entrepreneurial thinking among branch managers, preparing them to be agents one day. On the other hand, with an 80% agent / 20% branch split, this set-up can quickly overload branch managers. It is then better to rely on the district manager to make problem solving referrals on an ad hoc basis than set up such a system.

Recruitment

Recruitment criteria are the same for both internal and external candidates, but the recruitment process differs. The bank should have information on internal candidates in most areas, which one should check in case of external applicants.

In the case of external candidates, the recruitment process must include:

- Background / reference checks;
- Interviews by two layers of management;
- A numeracy / mathematical skills test;
- A sales skills case study test.

Otherwise, normal recruiting processes should be followed. That is, leads can be generated by advertising, using recruiters, personal or business contacts. HR needs to be involved. Benchmarks should be in place regarding the hiring process (e.g. not more than 10% of positions can be filled by interviewing and accepting a single candidate, all candidates scoring 80% or above for the position should be retained on file for future consideration, even if there is someone better to fill the specific opportunity at hand, etc).

The key factors to be considered for hiring / contracting decisions are:

- Proven financial resources to start up own business. Despite the start-up package provided by the bank, branch agents need to have their own resources to weather the first two to three years of operations, before they start earning substantial income;
- Supportive background, in terms of family, personal life, legal liabilities and similar. This is a tricky area as it is difficult to check for, due to privacy rules. However, experience shows that a supportive family background and lack of energy draining personal issues are a prerequisite for a successful start as an independent entrepreneur. In addition, branch agents should not be allowed to have any other contract with financial institutions, nor should they be allowed additional employment that would create a significant drain on their time;

- Entrepreneurial spirit. This means high energy levels, the ability to identify with the business, self-organisation, proactive problem solving, self-confidence in ability to overcome obstacles and a willingness to dedicate a substantial amount of time to building the business. (Experience shows that most successful branch agents do not take any time off for the first three years after staring their business.) A history of successful self-employment counts highly;
- Sales skills, business building ability. These include the ability to close sales, counter arguments and judge when to push and when to pull back. Pleasant, charismatic manners and the ability to identify customer needs are required. Candidates must have empathy for the customer tempered by an ongoing concern for running a profitable enterprise;
- Basic, technical, business skills of time management, operating under pressure, communicating clearly and convincingly, learning from own experiences, reliability and numeracy are required, along with a co-operative approach and the ability to build and manage teams;
- Financial services background. This is the most controversial area. Generally, this is more important at lower levels (e.g. sales agent – 75% importance), less important at the branch agent level (50% importance) and even less so if the bank starts the agent set-up above the branch manager level (25% importance). Experience shows that entrepreneurs without a financial services background tend to be more business focused but also less understanding of the unique control requirements of a bank. As a result, some organisations shy away from potential agent candidates without a financial services background, while others actively recruit them. The key point to keep in mind is that an absence of a financial services background should not automatically disqualify otherwise acceptable branch agent candidates.

Training

Before a new branch agent and staff are allowed to start operations they must participate in compulsory training, provided free of charge by the bank.

This basic essential training would normally take about two months for people unfamiliar with banking operations. Basic essential training includes:

- Use of technology;
- Banking regulations and legal aspects;
- Privacy, tax and money laundering;
- Product knowledge;
- Basic sales and servicing skills.

Once the basic essential training is satisfactorily concluded, the branch agent is allowed to start operating.

An additional month is usually required for initial mid-level sales training. This would include, for example:

- Objection handling;
- Prospecting (required at account manager level only);
- Closing deals (as above);
- Managing sales performance (for the agent only).

If the agent or his staff have banking experience (for example, a former branch manager and his employees) some or all of the above can be skipped. Some flexibility should also be built into the schedule, allowing for fast and slow learners. This usually results in a two- to six-month 'training window' within which a number of new branch agents can be qualified.

Refresher courses should be scheduled in advance. Also, when introducing new products or services both the agent and his staff (who would be involved in selling) should be required to be trained on them. Agreement on this point needs to be included in the agent contract to avoid potential disputes later. It is unacceptable for an agent not to train on a new product or service and choose not to offer it instead. This would contradict the 'uniform product offer across all outlets' approach that is paramount to running a successful mixed branch / agent sales network.

Risk management

Experience shows that there are nine specific risk areas that need extra attention (and prevention) among new branch agents. Some of these can be expected (such as credit related, general fraud), but some are harder to predict without actual experience in running a branch agent network. They are:

1. Higher than allowed deposit interest rates. Although branch managers sometimes also offer higher than allowed interest rates on customer deposits, experience shows this happens more frequently with branch agents. This is usually the direct result of the agent being part of the local community and having a closer personal relationship with potential depositors.
2. Ignoring the exclusivity clause of their contract. That is, working with, and offering products from, another financial institution, despite the contractual obligations of having to deal only with the bank. Typically this 'other' financial institution is a smaller bank with more attractive interest rates. Less experienced branch agents may not be able to counter rate-related arguments from prospects and feel forced to offer a third-party one-off deal to keep the overall customer relationship. More experienced agents may book the deal under their own name, redirect the funds to the customer and pocket the benefit of the rate difference.
3. Exchange rate games. Agents in areas of high currency exchange activity may try to benefit unethically in two ways. They may either try to guess rate movements and play them by building currency reserves. Or they may charge a different rate to customers from what the bank would for the same amount – to their benefit.
4. Unallowed activities. These would typically be activities related to financial services but not allowed by the bank, because the agent is not qualified to

carry them out and they take time away from banking activities. Typical examples would be real estate, tax, accounting and investment-related services. Note that this risk is highest early on after the start-up of a new branch agent outlet. It then tends to decrease rapidly as a new agent builds up his business and has no time for extra activities.

5. Mis-selling, especially higher-risk investment products. Branch agents may be tempted to sell customers whatever the customer thinks he wants, without following 'know your customer' rules or assessing the customer's risk tolerance. This can create negative customer reaction, bad PR and, in some cases, litigation risks.
6. False customer data entry. This normally happens when the agent wants to grant a loan and knows that the customer would not qualify. In an attempt to gain new customers and prove to the local community that they can 'arrange anything', younger agents may change customer information to be able to grant credit.
7. Fictitious loans – fraud. Loans may be applied by the agent for non-existent customers. Once enough funds are built up, the agent may disappear with them. Strong auditing, controls and systematised tracking of all funds advanced are needed to prevent this.
8. Paperwork. This cuts both ways. Younger agents, not used to the heavy documentation requirements of banks may be overwhelmed by paperwork, affecting their work, judgement, prudence. On the other hand, an agent may try to short-cut the heavy paperwork demand, creating regulatory and control risks. Close attention from the district manager is needed to mitigate these risks.
9. General negligence, especially among agents without previous banking experience. This could be as simple as keeping over-limit cash amounts on hand, ignoring safety keeping rules and similar issues. Nevertheless, they create unforeseen risks in the case of, for example, hold-ups or break-ins.

Control and audit

The five basic elements of audit and control which hold for traditional branches should also suffice for branch agents, although it may take special training for managers and auditors to effectively monitor the situation with the somewhat different agent set-up. As a standard, the following basic control and audit elements should be in place for branch agents:

1. Workflow checkpoints. Services and products can normally only be sold along pre-described workflows, which incorporate some control elements (for example, the 'four eyes principle' in which at least two people must witness or approve a certain activity). These workflows should be reviewed before starting up a branch agent network, keeping in mind the specific access and service rights of the agents and the risk factors described in the previous section.

2. Managerial control is usually exercised by the district manager, both on an ongoing and ad hoc basis. Again, the above risk factors need to be kept in mind. Also, special attention should be given to management efficiency within branch agent outlets, as many good agents are more entrepreneurial than disciplined.
3. Internal audit, compliance monitoring. This should cover not only regulatory, business risk and business process issues, but elements such as data protection and customer privacy issues to ensure a 360-degree review of all issues. Again, the thing to keep in mind is that branch agents are usually less compliance-oriented than branch managers and often treat regulatory activities as a waste of time – time taken away from useful sales activities.
4. Credit portfolio monitoring. The credit risk management and control processes in place are usually enough to control this area. However, given the specific risks mentioned in the previous section, extra diligence and attention is needed. It is also recommended that credit portfolio quality be tracked and analysed by each individual branch agent, even if all deals are approved centrally. 'Exception reporting' can often highlight a potential quality or fraud issue in time to take preventative action.
5. Service quality tracking. This can be done by a combination of quantitative customer surveys, mystery shopping and complaint tracking. Although this is an important element of performance management, experience shows it is not usually an area of concern with agents. Branch agents routinely score above the best branches for providing excellent customer service. This is because of their motivation to keep customers, their reliance on recommendations from existing clients and their pride in providing quality service in their local communities.

Legal / regulatory

The details of regulations for financial services intermediaries such as branch agents differ by country and, in some cases, even within the same country (for example, if financial services are regulated at individual state, province or territory level, instead of at federal level.) It is obviously mandatory that local laws and regulations be respected.

It is also advisable to work with the regulators from the outset. That is, discuss the plans to set up a branch agent network, explain your interpretation of local regulations and ask for guidance, help and ongoing consultation. It should never be assumed that the bank's interpretation of any regulation is exactly the same as that of the regulators. By working with the local regulatory agencies the bank ensures that the branch agent concept, when ready to be implemented, will be acceptable from a legal / regulatory perspective.

Contract

Overview

The contract document between the owner / entrepreneur (would-be branch agent) and the bank is the key piece that governs their relationship and respective rights, obligations and activities. It must be fully in line with local laws and regulations. It therefore reflects, to a large extent, those regulations. However, as a general guideline, it should contain:

- Duties and authorised activities of each party (both agent and bank);
- Exclusions;
- Remuneration;
- Scope of the contract.

Suggested areas to cover under each section are listed in the following sections. This list may not be comprehensive enough in all cases but should serve as a guide to start contract development activities. It should also serve as a checklist to ensure critical items are not omitted from this most important document.

Duties and authorised activities

- Description of the agent's activities and duties – what the agent is expected to do in terms of selling, servicing, business development; compulsory activities for the agent and his staff (e.g. training attendance), personal appearance, etc;
- Expected due diligence when conducting business on the bank's behalf – how to protect the bank's integrity when dealing with others on its behalf;
- 'When, how and about what' to inform customers, the bank and other parties – disclosure to customers and business partners, critical feedback to the bank about the business, competition, etc;
- Authorised representation of the bank – use of its name, signing on its behalf, making commitments, public comments and advertising;
- Control and responsibility for costs, taxes and similar;
- Confidentiality – both in terms of customer information and in terms of bank information;
- Ownership rules – who 'owns' the customer, their information, the product portfolios. Also, a clear statement about the bank's ownership of the so-called essential elements (listed under the 'Control' earlier in this chapter).

Exclusions

- No contract with, or activities for, other financial institutions or their agents and subsidiaries;
- No other business activities requiring more than 10% of the agent's time;
- No 'poaching' of customers from other bank outlets, be they branches or branch agents;

- Trade area definition (e.g. physical territory within which proactive prospecting is authorised), and business area definition (e.g. no corporate banking activities).

Remuneration

- Basis for remuneration – what is rewarded (e.g. portfolio volumes), what are the base essentials to qualify for payments (e.g. acceptable audit scores);
- Minimum sales objectives and targets if applicable, and minimum other requirements (for example customer service quality scores);
- Commission structure, including payment frequency and logistics;
- Who can change the commission structure and levels, when and how;
- Tracking both performance and payments – methods, control and frequency.

Scope of contract

- Time limit or indefinite expiry;
- Termination by either party:
  - Causes;
  - No cause termination;
  - Notice period;
  - Disengagement process, including:
    - Compensation for pending deals; and
    - Transfer of data from branch agent;
- Rules governing the selling or transferring of business, including:
  - Valuation;
  - Right of refusal by the bank (if any);
  - Bank approval needed (e.g. new agent);
  - What happens if the agent passes away;
- Extending the scope of contract:
  - New activities or business areas;
  - Additional outlets;
  - Lengthening time limit.

Commission

As outlined in the previous section, the general commission structure should be part of the contract. This, however, should not include the specifics of funds to be paid or the rates at which compensation may be set. It is advisable to have a separate

Commission Terms and Conditions paper, which is referred to in the contract and which sets out the specifics of the remuneration.

The Commission Terms and Conditions is another key element of the agreement between the branch agent and the bank. As the old adage goes: "You get what you reward – and you can only reward what you can measure." Structuring the commission system properly can drive the success or failure of a branch agent set-up, even if all other elements have been handled in the best possible way.

General commission design

The commission system must satisfy the following criteria:

- Simplicity – it must be easy to understand, track and verify;
- Driving results – it must reward the right behaviour to build a mutually profitable business for both the bank and the agent;
- Balance – between short-term and long-term business objectives, and between aggressiveness in building the business and prudence in managing risks;
- Flexibility – it must allow for changing the levels of remuneration without having to rework the commission structure itself, in order to respond to changes in the business environment.

Commission structure

Although a good general structure can be suggested based on experience with similar set-ups to date, it is useful to review the different options for designing a commission structure. This is because regulatory and business environments differ from one market to the next. My suggested structure may not be feasible under all circumstances. Therefore, the reader may need to modify it for best results, using one or more of the elements in the following sections.

Commissions can be upfront or ongoing, or a combination of the two.

Upfront commissions reward either specific activities or the results of those activities.

- As a rule of thumb, rewarding activities should be directed at sales staff with no bottom-line benefit from their efforts and limited control over their own activities. Branch agents do not fall into this category, so they should not be rewarded based on activities. However, they themselves should consider such a system for their sales staff;
- Upfront rewards for specific results make sense if the products sold do not provide ongoing revenue for the bank. Examples could be selling a third-party travel insurance or investment offer without a trailing fee;
- Upfront reward may also make sense to promote the right long-term behaviour. For example, a 'customer acquisition' reward for new clients ensures the agent will actively build a customer portfolio, which can be utilised later for cross-selling.

Ongoing commissions are based on the size of the business, for example the number of customers, portfolio volume, margin and fee income generated. As a general rule, they should reflect the success of the bank as closely as possible, without biasing against the agents. Therefore:

- Rewarding based on the number of customers is discouraged. Customers represent different levels of profitability. The agent should be encouraged to build a customer portfolio (with an upfront reward for new clients). However, he should then be encouraged to maximise profit on that portfolio by cross-selling to them. This would suggest ongoing reward based on portfolio volumes or similar criteria, not customer numbers;
- Rewarding simply based on product volumes is also discouraged. Different products represent different level of income to the bank. This should be reflected in the commission structure. However, care should be taken not to overcomplicate things and bias against the agents. The proposed route to take is to reward agents with a percentage of margins and/or fees, not with a percentage of profits. Margins are usually the result of the competitive environment, while profits are influenced by the bank's internal efficiencies (e.g. cost structure). There is more room for error in calculating profit figures. It may also penalise the agents for the bank's shortcomings.

Regardless of the upfront versus ongoing question, specific rewards can be structured in a number of different ways. Some examples are:

- Fixed – e.g. €20 per account;
- Variable – e.g. 0.5% of disbursed loan volume;
- Mixed – e.g. €20 per loan plus 0.3% of disbursed volume;
- Capped – e.g. €20 per loan, plus 0.3% of disbursed volume, up to €500 maximum (one-time or per year);
- Progressive – e.g. €20 per credit card sold for the first 10 each month, €30 for each additional card during the same month.

Key questions

In addition to the above variations, and in addition to the four key criteria listed for remuneration systems to satisfy, there are always additional questions related specifically to the branch agent approach. In my experience, the four most frequently asked questions (with proposed answers) are:

1. *Should we have minimum sales requirements below which we pay no commission?* No. Branch agents are extremely self-motivated. They only make money if they generate results. There is no additional 'squeezing' needed. Branch agents should have yearly plans and targets, but these should serve the purpose of planning the business well and allowing the district manager to help them achieve better results by reviewing, critiquing and supporting their plans.
2. *Do we need to check if the sale was 'real'?* Normally, no. What is usually meant here is if we need to check whether funds have been received into a deposit account opened, or the loan has been approved and successfully disbursed, or

similar. By designing a commission structure that rewards based on income generated on the actual portfolio, this extra check is already taken care of.

3. *Do we pay commission on items on which the bank makes no money?* No. However, this is mostly taken care of if calculating commission based on margin or fee income. A key exception is credit products, where commission should be suspended on part of the portfolio which is 90 days past due.

4. *How frequently can we change the commission structure?* As infrequently as possible, to avoid constant change in direction and avoid generating ill will among branch agents. Commission rates should be set for a 12-month period, in line with the yearly budget / planning cycle, then frozen at that level. The bank must retain the contractual right to change commission rates more frequently, to respond to exceptional changes in the business environment. However, by all means, the frequency of change should not average more than two per year in any three-year period.

Knock-out criteria

While it is recommended that no minimum sales criteria be set in order for branch agents to qualify for their commissions, some 'knock-out' criteria may be introduced. In addition to the credit quality-based criteria (see point 3 in the previous section), the most frequently used items are:

- Audit ratings;
- Customer service quality scores.

Minimum audit scores should be set and deadlines for improvements defined upfront. In extreme cases, commissions should be suspended until improvements are made.

Similarly, customer service quality should be tracked both internally (complaint tracking) and externally (mystery shoppers, customer research). Minimum expectations need to be agreed. A 'commission penalty' may be introduced if scores fall below certain levels. For example, no 'customer acquisition reward' until improvement is shown – but accumulated unpaid rewards are disbursed as soon as improvement is demonstrated. This approach motivates agents to make improvements quckly, to receive their funds.

Note that customer service quality should not be an issue with branch agents. They are very motivated to provide excellent service. Poor service quality scores should therefore be closely scrutinised to see if there are any systemic issues, unrelated to the agents' abilities, that drive scores down.

Sample commission structure

Below is a simple, well-tested commission structure that would satisfy all the requirements as discussed in this section. This could serve as a starting point to be modified as local requirements dictate.

The following are normally tracked monthly and commissions paid within 30 days:

- Deposit products – 45% of net interest margin (NIM);
- Lending products – 35% of NIM, 0% if payments are 90 days past due;
- Credit cards – 75% of yearly card fee. If no fees are charged, then 30% of NIM on outstanding balances. No commission of either kind if payments on outstandings are 90 days past due;
- Investments – 60% of front load charge (one-time) plus 30% of trailer fees
- Other third-party offer sales – 70% of fees paid to the bank by the third-party product provider;
- New customers – 10% of the bank's average direct acquisition costs (marketing and sales support only), one-time.

No commission is to be paid on:

- Selling features – 'features' are offers that do not exist on their own, but need to be linked to a product offer. For example, a debit card is a feature, because it needs a current account to which it provides access. An overdraft is a product, because it can exist on its own as a stand-by line of credit;
- Services – such as activating cards, address change, etc;
- Transactions – such as taking and paying out cash, unless it is a designated fee generating activity such as a wire transfer. In the latter case, 50% of fees charged is given as commission;
- Punitive charges – such as NSF (no sufficient funds) or similar.

Base-line expectations to qualify for remuneration are:

- Customer service quality scores in the upper 50% of network average. If scores fall below this, new customer acquisition commission is withheld until scores are improved back to upper-half standing. At that time, acquisition commission withheld is paid in full for the past 12 months (but not beyond);
- No audit ratings of 1 or 2 on a 1 to 5 scale, where 5 is best. Action plans presented within 30 days to address audit ratings of 3. Individual discussion with the district manager is initiated on all audit ratings below 4.

The above structure is set for a period of 12 months, starting with the yearly plan cycle. The bank reserves the right to change the structure with 60 days' notice if extraordinary business circumstances warrant.

Financials

Each financial institution should do its own financial modelling, using the templates agreed by management. However, a few guiding principles should be kept in mind:

- Financial calculations should be done both from the *bank's perspective* and from the branch agent's perspective. Both must show a viable business case for the new set-up to succeed;
- Comparisons should be done on a 'like for like' basis. Branch agent outlets are smaller than typical branches, which can bias results in their favour. On the

other hand, they are not allowed to handle corporate deals. This creates the opposite bias, if traditional bank branches are of a mixed, retail / corporate nature;

- Modelling should also be done on a 'channel portfolio' basis. That is, comparing the overall impact on the bank of opening agent outlets instead of traditional branches. It may take a different (higher) number of agent outlets to replace fewer, larger branches. This may be because agents are better suited to smaller communities than branches, or because they are smaller-sized outlets. Overall business dynamics should be explored and taken into account.

It should be fairly easy to estimate costs, based on the bank's experience with starting up and running branches, and based on the start-up package description provided for agents.

To estimate costs for the agent, it can be safely assumed that the agent would pay not more than 75% of the costs of a similar branch for goods and services. Employee costs can vary widely, as many agents use relatives and family members for cheap labour, in addition to putting in much longer hours themselves than a branch manager would. Finally, taxes need to be readjusted to reflect the breaks small businesses get in most jurisdictions.

Estimating revenues requires some judgment. Experience shows that branch agents would generate 35% higher revenues than corresponding same-size branches. This is partly based on a 20% higher cross-sell ratio, partly on higher customer retention (due to higher service quality) and partly on stronger focus on selling higher revenue products.

Individual product sales should be estimated based on local experience, but final figures should be compared back to the +35% revenue benchmark to see if they are in line. A branch agent outlet should have a break-even period of not longer than three years, either from the bank's or from the agent's perspective. If break-even is longer, the input parameters should be reviewed and changed if needed.

Comparisons

Table 2.1 shows indicative financial numbers, comparing an average bank-owned branch set-up (Model 1) with a corresponding agent set-up (Models 2 and 3). Because the agent set-up must make financial sense for both the bank sponsoring it and the independent agent, this set-up is reviewed from both these perspectives – hence the need for two models.

Note that total cumulative numbers for the agent set-up have been added in Model 2, combining both agent and bank figures. This is to make overall financial comparisons between agents and branches easier. (For an agent set-up, the combined costs / revenues of both the bank and the agent are comparable to the branch set-up – where only the bank's figures exist.)

Financial dynamics are shown for a mid-developed market environment in Europe.

Table 2.1: Indicative cost models

Model 1 – Branch dynamics from a bank's perspective

	Year 1	Year 2	Year 3	Year 4	Year 5	Cum 5yr
Revenue (fees + spread)	88	208	333	443	540	1,612
Cost of start-up package	nil	nil	nil	nil	nil	nil
Marketing / sales support expenses	29	26	22	20	13	110
Opex	193	200	231	238	271	1,133
P/L	-134	-18	80	185	256	369
Depreciation	38	38	38	38	38	190
Capex	384					384
Cash flow	-479	21	118	223	294	177
NPV (@approx. 12.5% discount rates)	-427	16	84	140	164	-23

Cum 'full 8 yr' NPV is 719

Model 2 – Agent dynamics from a bank's perspective

	Year 1	Year 2	Year 3	Year 4	Year 5	Cum 5yr	Agent's Cum 5 yr	TOTAL Cum 5 yr
Revenue (fees + spread)	56	147	238	314	377	1,132	896	2,028
Cost of start-up package	83	55	26	16	17	197	126	323
Marketing / sales support expenses	26	15	7			48	41	89
Opex	91	80	68	35	40	314	773	1,087
P/L	-144	-3	137	263	320	573	-44	529
Depreciation	19	19	19	19	19	95	95	190
Capex	363					363	20	383
Cash flow	-489	14	111	197	209	96	31	127
NPV (@approx. 12.5% discount rates)	-435	14	111	187	209	96	-8	88

Cum 'full 8 yr' NPV is 936

Model 3 – Agent dynamics from an agent's perspective

	Year 1	Year 2	Year 3	Year 4	Year 5	Cum 5yr
Revenue (fees + spread)	48	118	190	245	295	896
Cost of start-up package		13	25	44	44	126
Marketing / sales support expenses		6	11	13	11	41
Opex	109	125	142	184	213	773
P/L	-61	-26	12	4	27	-44
Depreciation	19	19	19	19	19	95
Capex	20					20
Cash flow	-62	-7	31	24	45	31
NPV (@approx. 12.5% discount rates)	-55	-5	18	12	22	-8

Cum 'full 8 yr' NPV is 194

Note: All costs in thousands of Euros
Best estimates "like-for-like" comparisons
Stress test as most expenses are front loaded
Models provided by 3-i Inc

Source: 3-i Inc.

Implementation

An expected time-frame for implementation is as follows, assuming branch agents would be integrated into an already existing, mostly traditional branch-based distribution system:

- Six months – to develop business plan, check for feasibility, obtain management approval (assuming no more than two weeks for decision and for authorisation to proceed);
- Six months – to start up first 10 agents, assuming no major extra time requirements for training and no bottlenecks in implementation (IT, regulatory, etc);
- Nine months – to monitor results and learn from pilot implementation;
- Three months – to incorporate lessons into roll-out plans;
- Six months – to start up next 10–100 agents.
- Sum total – 2.5 years from idea to large-scale roll-out, assuming disciplined approach to cover potential risks along the way.

A much faster roll-out is possible, but not advisable, as it may create unacceptably high business risks. This faster roll-out would still require a 12–18 month lead time.

The minimum time to start of roll-out is about 12 months, with an extra three to six months to implementation on a 50–150 agent scale. This would assume:

- Three months for feasibility checks, relying on all the information presented in this chapter;
- Three months to start up the first agents, using mostly internal candidates;
- Six months to test for downside effects of the set-up, before start of roll-out.

An even faster implementation is possible if a brand new business is being started up based on the branch agent concept. In that case, it should be possible to start up 100 branch agents within a year, provided that adequate resources are deployed to do so (and no external bottlenecks, such as unavailability of acceptable sites, interfere).

However, in this case, special attention is needed to ensure control remains with the ultimate business owner. This is because the bank may not be able to start up 'own branches' fast enough to address the critical point 4 of the requirements listed earlier under 'Control' (that 15–20% of outlets to be owned and controlled directly by the bank).

Summary

- The branch agent concept is a powerful way to improve efficiencies and create fast geographic coverage, cost efficiently, for a financial institution.
- It outsources many of the sales and service effort and shifts investment and personnel burden to local entrepreneurs, while keeping ultimate control with the bank.
- It therefore has many advantages over traditional branch-based coverage and can be speedily integrated into existing networks.
- It takes capital investments and headcount off the bank's books, creating additional flexibility.
- However, it needs to be controlled very carefully – substandard execution and ignoring control issues can be extremely (possibly fatally) costly.
- This chapter should have provided enough information for a practitioner to:
  - Form a preliminary idea about whether or not the branch agent concept would provide a benefit in his business environment;
  - Develop an outline and business case to be presented to management for discussion on the merits of such a set-up in the given environment;
  - Outline a detailed implementation plan, with 'to dos', cost and timing to allow fast start-up of the concept if management approval is received.

Case study 1: Volksbank's Romanian branch agent (branch franchise) set-up

By Robert Zanescu, public relations, communication, corporate affairs and social responsibility director, Bancpost, Romania

[Note that this was written in 2008, and therefore deals with activities in 2007, but as a case study it is highly relevant to this book. It is worth noting also that Volksbank has since risen from eighth to third bank in size by assets in Romania, which certainly demonstrates the continuing effectiveness of its set-up given the subsequent financial crisis.]

"Got sales experience and €20,000? Now you can have a bank of your own."

What does it take to be a banker in Romania? Well, the times when one should have had specific graduate studies with degrees that include bachelor's or master's in finance to be able to get the entry ticket for a career in banking are way gone. Check out the branch managers of several glass-and-steel eye-catching ING or Volksbank bank branches. What do they have in common? For sure, not many have studies in finance or banking. They are young, they have a strong sales track record, and they were willing to invest €20,000 in their future.

Every year on www.entrepreur.com, one can find the best of the most dynamic franchises. In the top 100 there are only seven franchises that operate in Romania: Re/Max – real estate; Pizza Hut – restaurants; Cartridge World – printer/fax cartridge replacements and sales; InterContinental Hotels Group – hospitality; McDonald's – restaurants; KFC – restaurants; and WSI Internet – internet business solutions and services.

The start was slow on the franchising market but now, since sales in almost every category (from FMCG products to durable goods and financial services) are skyrocketing, more and more Romanian business people are considering several options to go on their own – following their own idea or a borrowed one.

The banking sector experienced the same exponential growth as many of the other categories in Romania in recent years. Sales soared behind an extreme push on unsecured loans, credit cards, mortgage loans and home equity loans. The banks spread their distribution network at an unimaginable speed. To get more and more clients, banks opened branches at every major crossroad, not only downtown, but also in the remote areas of Romanian cities. These days one can access a bank branch as easily as a grocery store or a gas station.

The standard way of expansion for the banking industry was, and still is, the opening of fully owned branches. There are only two banks that dared to challenge the status quo and launched several branches in a franchise system: Volksbank and ING. It didn't take long for the results to show. As always in business, 'fortune favours the brave'. Five years ago nobody believed that without banking experience, having only a proven track record in sales, a strong desire to be on your own and a cash amount of the size of a mid-range car (€20,000) could be the beginning of a profitable and rewarding banking career.

Volksbank is a highly profitable bank. At the end of 2007 it reported an operational profit of €24.5m, 80% higher than the previous year, due to an increase in the number of loans given to its customers.

The bank's assets increased from €1.38bn at the end of 2006 to €3.5bn by December 2007. Over the same time its loan portfolio increased 170% to €2.21bn by the end of 2007, compared to €802m in December 2006. The bank's term deposits also grew 70% in 2007, reaching €530m by year-end.

These results made Volksbank eighth in the Romanian banking system by assets, with a market share of 5.06% at the end of 2007 – compared to a share of 2.71% in December 2006 (11th place).

These results were also due to strong distribution network expansion. In 2007, Volksbank expanded its network by 55 new units and grew the number partnerships in its franchising system by 40. The total number of sales outlets is 225, out of which 135 are Volksbank's own units and 90 are in franchise units.

Expanding the bank's operations has been always a priority for Volksbank. But at the same time, the bank planed to substantially grow its profits. These objectives seemed to be contradictory. However, CEO Gerald Schreiner had the means to do them both.

In previous years, Volksbank opened 50–60 sales outlets per year. The key challenge was indeed to combine network expansion with profitability. The bank's costs for growing its operations were quite low. Volksbank sales outlets were standardised and operation costs kept to a minimum. Industry forecasts showed that margins were declining, so the bank was getting ready to cut costs. Currently Volksbank can open a sales outlet for about half the cost of its competitors. An important contributor to this was Volksbank's commitment to expanding its network via the franchise system.

Building a franchise system was a bold thing to do, at a time when banks were not fully capable of moving their corporate culture towards a sales culture – the past kept them from considering sales as a part of service. Banks had an image of themselves as static service providers. Their idea of a business was to build as many sales outlets possible and wait for customers or, at best, advertise heavily on TV and in the press.

But Volksbank, and just a couple of other banks, understood that nothing happens until somebody sells something. This meant the start of a new era, a period when the focus was on how many customers a front-desk officer was able to generate per day or how effective the branch manager was in closing a small enterprise deal.

The franchise system was chosen to complement the quest for more customers and bigger profits. The financial investment for the bank is marginal; the outcome is generous if the franchise partner is an entrepreneur with a strong sales drive. All of this, together with continued support from the top management represented the key for profitable results. The net growth in income from the franchise system confirmed this.

The franchise system was not an idea restricted to Romania for Volksbank. The project was launched simultaneously in Romania, Hungary and other countries in the region. The challenges were two-fold:

- How to make sure that the customers will have the same shopping experience in the franchised outlets as they do in the Volksbank fully owned outlets; and
- How to induce the strong sales culture of the main bank, Volksbank, in the franchised branches.

One problem the Volksbank management encountered was that they didn't really know for certain if they had made the right decision about introducing the franchise system, until after the actual results came in. How did they actually determine if this method of increasing customer numbers and providing customer value at the same time was better than any other?

Evaluating the business impact of ideas can be complicated. To make it worse, there is an industry comprised of expert management consultants making it more complicated. But the Volksbank management kept things simple. They asked themselves if the franchise system was both meaningful and deliverable. If the answer to both was a 'yes', then they couldn't go too wrong in trying it.

So was it meaningful? The question was asked regarding both franchised partners and consumers. The reason for asking this question was to check if the franchise system was meaningful to the group of people that need to take action – the franchise partners to buy the franchise and run it profitably, and to the consumers to come to the Volksbank sales outlets in franchise system expecting the same benefits and banking experience as they did in the fully owned bank branches. The answer was yes, for both groups.

Volksbank is a respected name in the Romanian banking sector and the idea of being a partner of the bank was appealing to a large number of business people. If the branding and operational systems were to be implemented and monitored thoroughly, a franchised sales outlet had to deliver the same service level as a fully owned bank branch. The franchise idea also had to be meaningful to the bank itself, helping it achieve its goals and objectives. Resolving this question affirmatively helped eliminate one of the most damaging tools used before – discounts to drive customer acquisitions.

Of course, discounts are meaningful to the customer. A discount leverages increased volume via the value equation by reducing the cost denominator. But are discounts truly meaningful to the bank? Think again. Discounting to gain short-term volume is always an option, but it is seldom a good idea because it is one-sided in providing value. A good strategy is a win for the customer and a win for bank. And this is definitely what Volksbank did.

Was it deliverable? Could the bank do it, or not? It happens that some players rush out under competitive pressure and promise a meaningful benefit but they are not absolutely sure if they can deliver that benefit. Customers will seldom give them a second chance. Deliverability should be a fairly easy question in most businesses. The problem becomes not only whether Volksbank could actually do the meaningful things they promised (providing the same service level as in fully owned bank branches), but would consumers actually believe the bank could do it? Volksbank faced a cynical reality and figured it into its strategy: it under-promised and over-delivered.

The list of challenges for Volksbank was topped by planning and developing an organisational culture geared toward sales and positive results. Its sales-driven organisational culture is represented by basic assumptions, shared values and beliefs regarding the way Volksbank employees do things in their day-to-day activities. It is about how people will act under pressure, how decisions get made when a manager can't be around or about what is normal, what is rewarded and what it takes to 'survive'. The sales culture was to determine the way Volksbank put into practice the rules and the procedures of the bank and of the franchised partners.

Volksbank managed to create this sales culture by:

- Reward systems (variable and fixed payments to the staff);
- Employing empathic and transparent work styles of those in leadership or managerial positions. This is what many people say when asked what attracted them to work in Volksbank, either the fully owned bank branch or franchised branch: a transparent work style – an employee knows exactly where she or he is, what is required from she or him, and how the progress will be monitored.

Net/net, Volksbank is a successful case of how management could adhere to its principles and capture business growth in all distribution channels, fully owned or franchised, at the same time. What did it do consistently? It developed a vision for the future of the business and of the brand. It created strategies to support that vision. It then developed an integrated plan to implement those strategies. Last, but not least, it continuously learned, modified, then learned again and modified again.

The bank's success speaks for itself:

- A network of over 90 franchised branches in which their business partners invested €20,000–25,000 (some of the top performers in Volksbank's franchise system generate almost €3m in revenues);
- A boost in the sales of personal loans, car loans and mortgage loans (products that the franchised system is championing);
- A clear product portfolio that is always available to the consumer via motivated branch staff.

Case study 2: Branch franchising and kiosk combination by ING

Here is another case of using a branch agent model, although along 'converted franchise' lines, by ING – also in Romania. Note that ING has combined this with its 'Self'Bank' kiosk model, included at every franchise site. First, a review from ING's 'Shareholders Bulletin No. 2'.

Growth in emerging markets:

ING starts retail banking from scratch in Romania

Since July 2004, ING orange has become a real eye-catcher in shopping centres, business districts and residential areas across Romania. Sixty-three ING retail banking outlets in fifteen cities are now offering self banking services and personal finance advice. With their orange facades clad with the ING lion logo, they give ING further visibility in one of the promising emerging markets in Europe.

Starting the retail activities

Capitalising on ING's first mover status in the country and in response to the entrance, through acquisitions, of new foreign banks in Romania, ING launched the initiative of starting up retail banking operations from scratch. This was also in reaction to the growing need of the Romanian people for reliable banking and financing. Retail banking is a recent concept in Romania. Five years ago, mortgages for private individuals did not exist. Neither did credit card payments, ATMs and direct funds transfer. The plan for a greenfield in retail banking became concrete in 2003 and Dirk Serbruyns was appointed country manager: "Having to start without people, offices, PCs, ATMs and card technology brought out the true meaning of the word greenfield." With an abundance of energy, a local team was put together, office space was rented, storefronts were redesigned, machines were placed and people were trained. ING opened the first eight retail offices in July 2004.

The concept

The concept of the retail banking outlets in Romania is based on a combination of two concepts used at ING, the Self'Bank, known from our Belgian operations, and the franchising formula, adjusted to the local situation. Every office consists of two areas. One area is operated by ING Office Managers and the other is the Self'Bank area, offering clients the possibility to manage their accounts and finances. Located in the Self'Bank area are two innovative terminals specifically developed for the Romanian market, Bancomat+ and Multimat that offer step-by-step guidance and provide an easy way to pay bills, make bank transfers, make deposits or withdraw cash. Self'Bank is accessible seven days a week from 7 a.m. until 11 p.m.

During office hours, six days a week, clients can enter the staffed area of the bank and obtain information on mortgages, other banking products and purchase life insurance. This, too, is a revolutionary concept in Romania. The outlets are run on a franchise basis and the staff is not on the ING payroll. The office managers are former ING tied insurance agents who were retrained into all-round financial advisors.

An orange future

The dominant bright orange colour is making the ING retail banking offices with their Self'Banks highly visible. Serbruyns: "Romanians are starting to catch on to the self banking concept which is completely new here. Currently we have 85,000 active accounts and about one third of the transactions are now taking place outside regular office hours. By the end of 2005, we expect the number of outlets to have reached close to one hundred."

Indeed, Moody's February 2010 'Investors Service Report' notes that ING had 120 'retail outlets' in Romania, in addition to 24 'branches'. ING has not only reached its growth targets but exported the model to Poland as well, as reported at the 2009 ING Investor Day in Rotterdam by Eli Leenars, executive board member for the company. Good going!

Case study 3: Community banking, using the agent banking model in Australia

Bendigo and Adelaide Bank of Australia is providing banking services to remote communities by using what they call a 'Community Bank' set-up. This is very similar to the branch agent approach, but the local community takes equity participation in the outlet, instead of one single entrepreneur. Here is a description of how it operates, and a few words about its history, from the bank itself.

About Community Bank®

What is a Community Bank® branch?

A Community Bank® branch is a locally owned and operated company, which functions as a franchise of Bendigo and Adelaide Bank. Bendigo and Adelaide Bank provides the coverage of its banking licence, a full range of banking products, training of staff and ongoing support.

Depositors are protected by Bendigo and Adelaide Bank's imposing track record when it comes to the security of depositors' funds. We are one of Australia's oldest financial institutions, we have operated since 1858 and have declared a profit in every year and we have without fail honoured our depositors.

Bendigo and Adelaide Bank and the community company are each entitled to agreed portions of the revenue of the local Community Bank® branch and the local company is responsible for paying branch running costs.

When the local company begins to make a regular operating surplus, after the payment of branch running costs, and Bendigo and Adelaide Bank's share of the revenue is received, the remaining funds are available to be reinvested back into the community through dividends to shareholders and grants to community groups and projects.

The first Community Bank® branches

Between 1993 and 2000, more than 2,050 bank branches closed across Australia. These closures represented a 29% reduction in branch numbers in just seven years and many communities were left without branch banking facilities.

Bendigo Bank identified this trend and recognised the impact the reduction in branch numbers was having on communities.

The Community Bank® story first started in 1998 when Bendigo Bank partnered with the Victorian communities, Rupanyup and Minyip, to establish a banking pilot to return banking services to the towns. It succeeded, and since the twin branches inception a decade ago, more than A$450,000 in profits has been channelled back into community projects.

Growth of the network

When it first started, Community Bank® was eagerly sought out by many rural communities looking for a sustainable solution to branch banking that could be quickly implemented, but the model has proven to translate into metropolitan communities and is now one of the fastest growing banking networks in Australia.

The number of Community Bank® branches has doubled in the last four years and in the same time frame, customers have tripled their commitment of banking business to the community network, increasing it to more than A$16.3bn.

More importantly, in excess of A$40.3m in Community Bank® branch profits has been returned to community projects and A$14.7m has been paid in dividends to more than 63,000 local shareholders.

And behind those numbers are hundreds of stories of Community Bank® branches making a real difference to the lives of local people.

Whether it's building a community hall, sponsoring an art prize or even buying new footy jumpers for the local side – these Community Bank® branches are helping improve the economic and social prospects of their local communities.

Add to those contributions the employment of more than 1,100 staff members and daily expenses in the local economy and you have a truly meaningful contribution to those communities and to local prosperity.

At the end of March 2010 the Community Bank® branch network had achieved	
Community Bank® branches	255
Donations to local groups and projects	A$40.3m
Volume footings	A$16.3bn
Shareholders	63,332
Dividends paid to shareholders	A$14.7m
Community Bank® branch staff	1,152
Community Bank® branch directors	1,690
Community Bank® accounts	788,218

The future

Today, there are more than 255 Community Bank® branches right across Australia from Alice Springs in the Northern Territory, Augusta in the West and Dover in Tasmania.

The essence of the Community Bank® concept is in sharing the responsibilities and rewards between the community and our bank. Communities across Australia have accepted the responsibility of providing start-up capital and making their branches successful – and are increasingly reaping rewards that aren't just limited to banking.

In the early days, most attention was focused on how the Community Bank® concept has secured face-to-face banking services for local communities. Of course this is important, but it ignores the tremendous social and economic contributions being made by Community Bank® branches as more capital is retained locally, more commercial activity is stimulated and the confidence of local community leaders increases.

We continue to witness the tangible results produced by the Community Bank® model – not just in rural areas, but in our regional centres and the suburbs of our capital cities.

Bendigo and Adelaide Bank continues to participate in the development of the Community Bank® model with an enormous sense of pride. We are indeed fortunate to partner with many vibrant and successful communities.

The success of the Community Bank® network in its first decade indicates that the sky is the limit for communities that choose to realise the ambitions they have for the economic security of their residents and businesses.

Chapter 3

Sales agents – single-minded focus on acquisition efficiencies

Overview

Sales agents are sometimes also called mobile bankers, direct sales agents, business development officers, outreach sales force, or similar. Used correctly they can add significant acquisition power to an existing physical distribution system. The model discussed in this chapter is one of 'outsourced but controlled help'. That is, when sales agents are not employed but contracted by the bank and are not loaned from a sales brokerage outfit but work exclusively for the bank. This is a powerful set-up, which has several advantages in terms of flexibility, cost and control.

As in the previous chapter, general descriptions of concepts and benefits are followed by functional headings to allow the practitioner to set up and run such an agent network based on the knowledge presented. In addition, a few key attachments are also provided. Importantly, guidelines and templates for drafting contracts are included. Because sales agents are a more thoroughly tested model and fit better within standard regulatory frameworks, the danger of providing unacceptable templates is much lower than in the case of branch agents. Hence the templates provided for sales agents but not for branch agents.

Definition

Sales agents are commissioned, acquisition-focused, mobile (outreach) sales individuals. They are not bank employees, but individual entrepreneurs who have an exclusive contract with the bank to sell its products, focusing on generating new customers.

A more detailed definition of sales agents is:

- Self-employed individual persons, with an exclusive contract either with the bank or with a purposely set-up agency owned / controlled by the bank. They can only sell the products approved by the bank and cannot represent any other financial institution;
- They focus on acquiring new customers for the bank, initiating the future customer's relationship with the bank (hence, usually having only a one-time relationship with prospects / customers);
- Their focus is on upfront product sales, rather than cross-selling or relationship building. No after-sale service is to be performed by sales agents, except the basic essential, mandatory follow-up to ensure the product sale has been concluded satisfactorily (verification of funds received or disbursed, follow-up call to customer);
- Remuneration is commission based for individual product sales, rather than on portfolio volumes as in the case of branch agents;
- Sales agents are usually linked to bank sales points, branches or branch agents for:
    - Cross-referrals (e.g. closing leads which the branch staff are unable to follow up on and passing over deals they are not authorised to handle); and

  - Easier sales execution (e.g. dropping off account opening forms);
- However, they are managed centrally;
- Sales agents have limited authority to represent the bank:
  - They can present and accept contracts but cannot approve them or input them into the bank's system;
  - They cannot open accounts or grant loans – this needs to be done either centrally or by bank sales points with authorisation;
  - Sales agents cannot accept or pay out cash;
  - They cannot sign on the bank's behalf (except signing for receipt of an account opening form or loan application or similar);
- Sales agents only have a limited product range they are allowed to sell;
- Sales agents should not provide any ongoing customer service;
- They are not allowed to delegate their sales tasks further. That is, they cannot hire or contract people to delegate activities to;
- They are supported by central marketing activities but are expected to do their own local business development;
- They must use their own premises, which cannot appear as a branch or agent outlet. However, they may have some common work area set aside on bank premises or in some physical outlets.

Different concepts

There are many variations of the sales agent concept.

- 'Outreach sales force' and 'business development officers' usually refer to bank employees who are expected to work out of the office to acquire new customers for the bank. They may be heavily commissioned, but they are not self-employed individuals. They also, usually, have full representation rights for the bank – they can sign on the bank's behalf.
- 'Sales agents' and 'direct sales agents' may cover different set-ups:
  - They may have a contractual relationship (either self-employed or employee) of an alliance partner of the bank, such as an insurance company or credit card monoline business. As part of the alliance deal between the bank and its partner, they may be allowed (and requested) to sell the bank's products as well, in addition to their own company's offers;
  - They could be hired through an agency set up by the bank for the sole purpose of developing and managing such a sales force for the bank. Whether sales agents are hired directly by the bank, with individual contracts, or through a separate agency, will usually be driven by legal, regulatory and cost considerations. If it is better for the bank to set up a separate agency to contract individual sales agents to work for the bank, the bank may do this in two different ways:

(i) Taking an equity (usually a majority) participation in the agency; or

(ii) Having an exclusive central contract with the agency owned by others.

If the bank does not own a majority stake in the agency, then the central contract needs to be carefully worded, to ensure exclusivity for the bank and preventing the agency from selling the services of its sales agents to others;

- 'Mobile bankers' can refer either to bank employees or sales agents contracted directly or via a central agency;
- 'Brokers', 'representative sales force' or sales agents branded under a name different from the bank, normally mean a non-exclusive arrangement with a third-party company over which the bank has limited influence. These third parties may have a broker network or a sales force for hire. Contracting these outfits should be done with extreme care and limited expectations. This is because:
  - They are usually experienced in selling insurance and investment products but have limited experience in selling basic banking offers;
  - Because commissions on standard banking offers also tend to be lower than insurance / investment offers, these hired sales forces usually lack the motivation to push the bank's offers;
  - Most of these firms wish to own the customer relationships, which prevents long-term value generation to the bank.

This chapter deals with the sales agent set-up proven by experience to be the most beneficial to most banks: sales agents who are not bank employees but are contracted either directly or via an agency set-up controlled by the bank. This set-up will add an important distribution channel that is:

1. Designed for proactive customer acquisition;
2. Flexible;
3. Strictly sales focused;
4. Cost-effective / cost-efficient;
5. Product dedicated.

Benefits

Experience has shown a wide range of benefits from using sales agents to compliment physical outlets and other, remote channels. Note that many of the benefits listed here can also be used as benchmarks to set expectations towards sales agent networks:

- Extra sales – up to 50% of new customer acquisitions can easily be generated through sales agents and should be a target when setting up such a channel. On a product basis, up to 80% of new sales can be achieved (for example, credit cards), especially if the market is not yet developed enough to allow alternative direct sourcing or has regulatory barriers to direct marketing. The latter is the case in many new EU member states where direct marketing may not have had a chance to develop to Western European levels before strong EU data protection laws made new contact list generation near impossible;

- Lower cost of acquisition – between 15% and 50% of standard direct sourcing costs. Experience suggests sales agents should be able to generate new product sales to prospects between €25 and €75 per sale, depending on the product (Western European cost scale). This compares with regular direct sourcing costs (allocated marketing and sales support only) of between €50 and €500 for matching products;
- Better control – better cost control because commissions are only paid for confirmed product sales. This allows for more rigorous marketing and sales support budget planning. There is also better control over product portfolio build-up. Sales agents are focused on a limited product range and can be easily directed towards selling specific offers – for example, credit products if higher margin revenues are needed or deposits if liquidity needs to be increased. Simple changes in the commission structure can quickly and efficiently accomplish this, without disrupting the yearly plan of the less flexible branch network;
- Flexible set-up – one can quickly add coverage to existing networks, enter new markets and scale up acquisition / product sale power if market conditions demand. Similarly, if conditions dictate, a sales agent network can be scaled down much faster, at a lower cost and with fewer complications given its contracted (as opposed to employed) workforce;
- Consumer demand – most consumers still prefer face-to-face contact (as borne out by most research on the topic of channel usage and preferences), even while wanting the flexibility and convenience of not having to visit a branch for all their needs. In addition, most people feel more comfortable discussing their borrowing needs outside of the 'intimidating' branch environment;
- Sales process fit – some products are sold, not bought. Credit cards are a prime example. A face-to-face direct selling approach works well for credit cards, especially in markets where they are not yet fully accepted (essentially, outside the Anglo-Saxon environment). A direct-selling sales agent network is often needed to build a credit card portfolio. Citibank's success in using this approach to penetrate emerging markets with credit cards is but one example of this;
- Internal experience, benchmarking, control – it is highly recommended that any financial institution set up its own sales agent network before entering into a contract with third-party sales support providers (brokers, 'sales force for hire' and similar set-ups). This will let the institution learn about managing such a sales force and setting sales targets for them. It will send a signal to the other party that the bank knows what it is doing and has well-founded performance expectations, based on its own experience. It also provides a back-up in case something goes wrong with the relationship and extra sales are needed to keep sales on track.

The following two case studies come from my experience in working with two mid-sized banks that have implemented sales agent networks, along the lines recommended here. Case study 4 was a time-limited promotional test at one branch only. Case study 5 deals with an ongoing set-up, on a national coverage basis of 30 branches and 300 agents.

Case study 4: Limited promotional sales agent test

Bank A wanted to test the upside potential of implementing proactive retail sales processes in a universal branch banking set-up. It ran a pilot in a branch that won the right to it via internal competition (hence motivation was assured). The basic set-up prescribed layering in a new, proactive sales process, in support of specific goals.

The set-up involved:

- Building on sales training already completed;
- Planning to use excess branch capacity;
- Assuming that sales basics were in place, as claimed.

Key elements of the proactive sales approach included:

- Local follow-up on central marketing events;
- Personal sales calls to prospects mailed centrally;
- Corporate employee acquisition activities;
- Proactive offers to walk-in prospects;
- Proactive, personal cross-selling to selected branch customers.

Table 3.1 shows the results, in terms of portfolio growth during the test period and during the same period the previous year (base).

Table 3.1: Portfolio growth

	Base period	Test objective	Test results
Test location	+7%	+46%	+21%
Control location	+10%	+15%	+13%

Source: 3-i Inc.

Initial evaluation of the results produced an unclear picture. While the test location under-achieved its objective, this could have been the result of over-aggressive target setting without adequate business and capacity planning. The point was made that growth at the pilot site was still much higher than at the control location. This picture changed when results were broken out by sales agents, affiliated with the locations, and by branch staff. Filtering out sales agent numbers from the test results is shown in Table 3.2.

Table 3.2: Portfolio growth without sales agents

	Base period	Test results, w/o sales agents
Test location	+7%	+8%
Control location	+10%	+12%

Source: 3-i Inc.

This shows that 13% of the total of 21% growth at the test site came from sales agents, not from branch staff. Branch sales people at the test site performed no better with the new set-up and extra support than their counterparts at the control site. Strong increase in sales agent results accounted for essentially all of the sales improvement. Sales agents responded strongly to the opportunities presented and took advantage of the extra support.

Follow-up tests showed that results are much poorer at locations where sales agents are not linked to actual physical outlets. Key conclusions included the need to integrate all sales-related elements (including training, capacity planning, proactive sales processes, etc). They also included the need to link sales agents to branches and branch agents to allow them take advantage of central support activities better.

Case study 5: Ongoing national sales agent test

The findings from Case study 4 above can be explained by looking at the sales dynamics figures, as measured at another bank ('Bank B'), across a mid-sized branch network (30 branches) with a mid-sized sales agent group (300 agents) linked to them. The dynamics shown in Table 3.3 should be read in the context of the explanations that follow it.

Table 3.3: Bank sales network dynamics

		Branch staff	Sales agents	Agent / staff index (%)
No. of credit products sold per month		5	15	300
No. of deposits products sold per month		8	10	125
Total no. of products sold per month		13	25	192
Of which, sold proactively:	No.	3	25	833
	%	23	100	435
Percentage of time spent on active selling		20	80	400
Estimated max. % that could be spent selling		45	85	189
No. of products per month sold if max. time achieved		14	27	193

Source: 3-i Inc.

The data in Table 3.3 clearly show the benefits of using sales agents for focused product sales and customer acquisitions. Note that their higher efficiency does not mean that branch staff are just 'lazier'. To a large extent it reflects the different set-up and focus of sales agents: no servicing; no handling of cash; limited administrative duties.

The numbers also should not be taken to suggest that an effective overall sales distribution network can rely on sales agents alone. Customers need the convenience of full product offers and full servicing provided by branches, the reassurance of brand presence (bricks and mortar), and they appreciate the convenience of anytime banking through the internet and call centres.

The following reviews what some of the lines represent in Table 3.3:

- 'Number of credit products sold per month' – this is higher with sales agents because they were incentivised to sell those products. As mentioned previously, simple commission changes can drive agent sales behaviour quickly and efficiently. Also, selling credit products requires a proactive approach for which the sales agent has more time and which he is motivated to pursue aggressively.

- 'Number of deposit products sold per month' – this is much closer between the two groups, as many of these products are sold on a 'per request' basis to walk-in prospects in the branches.
- 'Number of products sold proactively' – reflects 100% of the total number sold for sales agents, as every single sale is a proactive one for them. It is a much lower percentage for branch staff, reflecting their different duties (e.g. cashiers), more time spent on servicing and their heavier administrative burden.
- 'Percentage of time spent on active selling' – also reflects the above. Note that time spent on prospecting is included in 'active sales time'.
- 'Estimated maximum percentage of time that could be spent selling' – assumes one takes away all tasks that can be removed from each group, to free up more time for selling. The relative increase would be much smaller for sales agents (from 80% to 85%), because their service and admin burden is already very low.
- 'Number of products that could be sold per month if maximum percentage sales time is achieved' – is how many products branch staff and sales agents, on average, could sell if they spent the respective 45% and 85% of their time on proactive selling. For branch staff, for example, the '14' figure is calculated as follows: 45% is divided by 20% to get the increase in time available for proactive selling. The resulting 2.25 increase factor is then multiplied by 3 (the number of products currently sold proactively) to give 6.75, the new 'proactively sold number of products per month'. At the same time, the current reactively sold number of products (10 per month) needs to be reduced in line with the reduction of time left for reactive selling and other duties. This is done by dividing 55% (the new 'reactive time') by 80% (the previous 'reactive time'), giving a 0.69 factor. This is then multiplied by 10, the number of reactive sales, to result in 6.9. By adding this 6.9 figure to the 6.75 figure one gets the approximate 14 figure shown.

It is important to note how closely this correlates with results from Case Study 4, from Bank A, in another market. Case Study 4 showed that layering in proactive sales processes (and some additional sales time) did not significantly improve branch-based sales. The sales dynamics review conducted at Bank B suggests that these findings should not have been unexpected. To significantly improve branch-based sales one needs to follow an integrated sales boost approach. Simply freeing up more time 'for selling' will not increase results.

(More can be found on ways to boost sales in an integrated way in Volume 1 of this series, 'Sales and Sales Management in Financial Services: A Hands-on Guide to Global Best Practices'.)

Products

Number of products

As described earlier, sales agents should not offer the full product range the bank has to offer. A more restricted product range focuses their attention better and improves efficiencies. The number of products found to be ideal for sales agents to sell is two to four. In exceptional cases, and after considerable experience, five to six products may be acceptable. 'Considerable experience' here means three to four years of demonstrated success with sales agents, a stable HR situation and a well-documented knowledge base.

Sales agents can start with only one product if required. Additional products are then added, as the agents become familiar with selling their first product, so adding another does not jeopardise their sales efficiency on the previous one. As a rule of thumb, a new product should never be added less than six months after introducing the previous one.

There is often strong push from product managers to add their products to the sales roster of sales agents on accelerated timing, in greater numbers. This should be resisted. Adding new items too fast can destroy efficiencies already built up. Adding too many offers will do the same.

Another common issue at many banks is 'mobile sales force proliferation'. This is usually the result of pressure from separate, product-based, strategic business units (SBUs) to have their own, dedicated, outreach sales force. This can result in having multiple sales agent networks, or a combination of sales agents, bank employee mobile bankers, third-party agents, etc. Again, this proliferation should be resisted as much as possible. Sales agents need to fit within the overall strategy of the bank. What they sell and do not sell should be prioritised and agreed – and then enforced enterprise-wide.

Types of products

The first product sales agents sell is usually one of the following:

- Credit cards – the credit card sales process ('push') fits well with the sales agent business development style. Credit cards are also good initial acquisition products. They can be sold and serviced remotely. They provide a good source of data (transactional, credit) to allow further, targeted, cross-selling.
- Mortgages – initial mortgage discussions are time consuming and can tie up branch capacity. In addition, many prospects would rather discuss their mortgage-related needs away from the 'threatening' branch environment. Finally, mortgage selling is often facilitated by intermediary contacts – real estate agents, realtors – for whom the convenience of having someone able to help them on a sales site is paramount. A mobile, outreach mortgage sales force is therefore usually the answer. Some of these sales forces may use the sales agent set-up instead of utilising employees.
- New, innovative, deposit or investment products – many of these products can easily be copied by the competition and it is important that maximum sales coverage be given to them before that happens. Because they provide unique benefits, they can be a relatively easy sale. Banks with limited physical distribution often introduce such new products relying on sales agents for quick volume build.

Additional products

This will depend on several factors. In the case of a sales agent network started up with mortgages, the chances are they will stay focused on mortgage sales alone. This is because of the specialist knowledge required, with a lengthy sales process but high-value sales, especially if working with intermediaries. As a result, the next products would usually be limited to those tied to mortgages, e.g. insurance offers and current accounts for payments.

In case of other sales agents, personal loans are often the second offer added. This is partly because of their higher margins, and partly because standard accounts and deposits are relatively easily sold, in a reactive way, through branches and branch agents.

However, as mentioned before, the product mix needs to fit within the bank's strategic needs and should be agreed overall. For example, liquidity needs may dictate a deposit focus, despite the arguments put forth above, for selling personal loans. In addition, care should be taken that the product mix offered is a logical one from the customer's perspective. Otherwise the sales efforts of the agents will be undermined. For example, credit cards, personal loans and current accounts fit well together. Credit cards, retirement investments and mortgages do not.

Product sales process

Sales agents are responsible for targeting the right segments in their business development activities (e.g. based on income, age, employment, etc). They are also responsible for the first round of document verifications – signatures, income and similar. Their responsibilities are included in their contracts and their compliance with the responsibilities is verified by their direct managers. They are also responsible for truthful representation of the bank's offer and help their prospects through the sales process at a high quality service level. Appendix A at the end of the chapter provides a sample of 'prospect contact rules' for this area. These should normally be attached to the general contract between the bank and the sales agent.

Services

Given the strict acquisition / product sale focus of sales agents, they are not expected (and not allowed) to provide most of the services available through other sales or service channels. Sales agents should not be able to change customer information in the bank's operating system or customer files. Their services should focus on what is described above under 'Product sales process'. After-sales service should be restricted to a follow-up call to the prospect, 14 days after a product sale was initiated. They should check if everything has gone well, account opened, funds disbursed, etc. They should also explore any potential extra customer needs, to be addressed either by themselves or (more likely) to be referred to an authorised channel for follow-up.

IT support

Because of the limited product offering, and because sales agents provide essentially no services and no representation of the bank in terms of opening accounts or similar processes, there is limited additional IT support required for a sales agent network. Key requirements for IT support include:

- Remote access to company product information for products sales agents can offer;

- Document (forms) retrieving, information input (filling out electronic forms), printing and document transference capability to initiate account opening or credit request;
- Email and mobile phone messaging systems;
- Tracking mechanism to:
  - Allocate product sales to individual agents and their supervisors;
  - Verify product sale (e.g. funds in the account or loan disbursed);
  - Allocate commission and track / verify its disbursement.

Other support

Start-up – there is no special start-up package as is the case for branch agents. The compensation system should allow for an upfront cashflow guarantee, in the form of a fixed salary for an initial period (e.g. three months). This will be detailed later, as part of the commission system review.

Marketing – sales agents benefit from central marketing activities but are expected to do their own business development and pay for it themselves.

Training – provided free of charge and is mandatory. This is discussed in greater detail later in the chapter.

Premises – a work area may be provided in a branch or branch agent outlet that a sales agent is affiliated with, but agents are expected to work from their own premises or at the prospect's location.

Sales – coaching and supervision are available from more senior supervisors and managers, some independent, some bank employees. This is discussed under 'Organisation' later.

Control, risk management, audit

Sales agents have a limited scope of activities, no access to the system, no significant delegated authority and clearly defined expectations, agreed in a binding contract at the individual level. As a result, the special control and risk issues presented by branch agents do not apply. Sales tracking, administration and information verification are key areas. They should be addressed via the right organisational design, IT system and contract wording.

However, critical success factors and risk / control areas related to the sales agent set-up can be summarised as follows:

1. Focus must be on new customer acquisition and one-time product sales. Anything else should be left to other channels. Therefore, the whole set-up must be geared towards a single-minded, short-term, product selling objective. This includes organisational set-up, IT support, commission system, audit rules and more.
2. The product range offered for sale must be narrow – not the full range available through other channels. Service offerings must be eliminated or

severely restricted. Strict controls must be in place to enforce adherence to this principle.

3. Sales agents must be closely controlled. The focus is on short-term results. Agents cannot decide what they should and should not be able to sell. Rewards for good performance, and punishment for lack of performance, should be quick and transparent to all.

4. The processes employed must be simple – sales focus, rewards, acceptable and unacceptable behaviour, acceptable and non-acceptable sales will all drive sales agents towards the required behaviour. They should always know what to do and what gets rewarded.

5 Sales reported must always be confirmed and verified. Commissions and other payments should only be advanced when the sales claimed by agents actually benefit the bank. Special attention should be paid to tracking:

   a. Fictitious accounts;

   b. Dormant accounts;

   c. Credit requested but not drawn / disbursed;

   d. Credit requested but not approved;

   e. Products requested but not activated (or credit cards not picked up).

6. The downside of activities must be planned for and covered. Dismissals, fraud and high turnover are part and parcel of a sales agent set-up and must be managed as part of the business.

7. Sales agents are the face of the bank and this should never be forgotten. Seemingly mundane and innocuous things such as dress codes and acceptable behaviour should be regulated and be part of the contract.

8. Sales agents should focus their activities on high potential target segments. Because many of the agents do not have a strong business background, this focus should be mandated from the bank's perspective. For example, specific definitions for prospects to be approached should be part of the sales agent job description. Credit risk criteria should be part of the definition whenever sales agents are selling lending products.

9. Sales agents must be integrated into the bank's overall multi-channel line-up. Roles and responsibilities must be defined in the overall context of the bank's delivery channel strategy.

10. Strong aided brand awareness is a must to make the sales agent set-up work. Therefore, marketing strategies must be brought in line with the existence of this sales channel. Unaided brand awareness normally helps branch walk-in traffic, because it puts the bank's name in customers' minds when they may be thinking about a new banking relationship. Unaided brand awareness prompts recognition of the bank's name when mentioned to them. This is crucial when, for example, a sales agent calls and mentions he is representing a certain financial institution. If the person called has an awareness of the bank mentioned, he will listen. If he does not, he is likely to hang up.

Therefore, marketing strategies and spending allocations must be altered to accommodate new channels such as sales agents. (The same goes, by the way, for any other direct acquisition-focused channel set-up.)

Organisation

As described earlier under 'Definition', sales agents should be linked with physical outlets if possible, but managed centrally. This means a layered organisational structure, where sales agents are managed by team leaders, who in turn report to senior team leaders (titles may vary, roles usually do not). At the same time, sales agents and their managers / leaders matrix to the physical channel structure as shown in Figure 3.1. One could replace 'branch managers' with 'branch agents', but then the dividing line between 'bank employees' and 'contract hires' would have to be redrawn.

Figure 3.1: Organisational structure – integrating sales agents and their managers

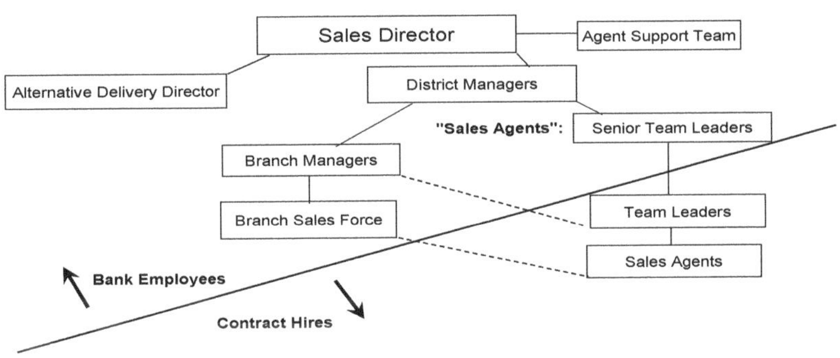

Source: 3-i Inc.

Figure 3.1 shows the vertical management structure, local links and support function. It gives a possible structure which may change based on the development stage of the network and the business. Specifically, the district manager and senior team leader functions may overlap, especially at the early stages of setting up. In that case, they may be collapsed into one. In addition, senior team leaders may be kept as contract hires, although this is not recommended.

The different positions can be summarised as follows:

- Sales agents are self-employed, product sales / customer acquisition-focused individuals, paid for short-term performance. They liaise with sales staff at the bank's outlets and report to team leaders;
- Team leaders are also self-employed, each managing 8–12 sales agents, in addition to being engaged in direct selling themselves. They are compensated for their own sales results, for the results of their team and for handling their sales management / administrative duties properly. They report either to a senior team leader or to a district manager;

- Senior team leaders should normally be bank employees, each managing 8–10 team leaders. They do not engage in personal selling but manage the development of the sales agent network for their territory. Their compensation should be heavily based on the results of their teams. In the early stages of the sales agent network development this position may not be needed and the duties filled by district managers;
- The support team is a central function, to provide sales management and administration support as needed. For greater efficiency, this function should support both branch agents and sales agents if a bank has both of those channels. One would need 5–10 employees in the support team (one of whom would be the manager) for a sales agent network of 400–500 individuals, including agents, leaders and senior leaders.

Roles and responsibilities

Sales agents:

- Sales;
- Sales; and
- More sales...

Team leaders:

- Manage team of sales agents – daily coaching, cultivating branch relationships, conflict resolution, sales motivation, responsibility for team's results;
- Administration – verification of account and credit applications, initiation of administrative requests (to support team or senior leader) as needed;
- Personal sales – especially 'block acquisitions', targeting larger groups of prospects such as employees of corporate accounts.

Senior team leaders:

- HR management – managing team leaders, recruiting, personnel issues, team building. Due to the high flexibility of the sales agent set-up and relatively high turnover rates, the senior leader is normally expected to be able to hire up to 10 new sales agents per month and handle up to five termination cases;
- Business development – for the territory, including responsibility for direct sales results, capacity planning, liaising with other business units of the bank as needed, tracking efficiency, quality, suggesting direction of business development efforts of teams;
- Administration – ensuring high quality commission settlement process and sales tracking, follow-up on compensation issues as needed, training management, termination cases, compliance issues.

Support team:

- Central sales management and administration, including:
  - Contract drafts, archiving, tracking, assigning agent codes, dismissal cases (notices, final commission, legal review, archiving);
  - Compensation management, calculating and disbursing commissions, salaries, bonuses;
  - Sales verification, deals tracking, verifying active accounts or loan disbursements, funds in / out, customer verification if needed, reporting;
  - Expense management, expense accounts for training and other justified activities, ordering equipment (e.g. mobiles), cost reimbursements (e.g. car mileage if in contract), returned equipment;
  - Other, including training co-ordination, business cards, materials, forms, liaising with external accounting and other firms, service quality follow-up calls, etc.

Career progression

Despite the fact that sales agents are individual entrepreneurs on contract only, it is useful to plan career progression for them. This provides extra motivational value to the agents and ensures a better supply of good quality sales persons and managers for the bank. The usual career progression for a sales agent would be first to team leader, then to senior team leader. At the senior team leader level he would normally be offered permanent employment by the bank. If he does not want to give up his self-employed status he should be considered as prime talent for becoming a branch agent (if the bank has that channel).

Training

Training should be both mandatory and provided free by the bank. It should be part of the recruitment / start-up process and be included in agent contracts to ensure understanding of expectations in terms of attendance and compliance with expectations. Training can be broken into two parts: start-up and ongoing.

No agent is allowed to start work without undergoing start-up training and passing it at an acceptable level.

It is recommended that, at some point, ongoing training is separated into two tracks: one for regular sales agents and one for potential high performers who are being considered for the next level up. This helps talent management and provides extra motivation for sales agents.

A typical training programme is shown below.

Start-up training

- Orientation:
  - Three to five days' duration;

- Basics about the bank, its culture and set-up;
- Managing the system and administration;
- Information on the products the agent is allowed to sell;
- Roles and responsibilities of the agent and his contacts.

- Sales basics:
    - Three days' duration;
    - Product benefits and features;
    - Handling objections;
    - Closing;
    - Follow-up.

Ongoing training

- Basic refresher:
    - One day every three months;
    - Sales skills practice;
    - New promotions coming;
    - New products added to the selling list;
    - Update on the bank and major trends affecting the business.
- High performers:
    - One additional day every six months;
    - Sales management skills (e.g. coaching, motivation);
    - Sales administration (e.g. sales tracking, budget management);
    - Other products and offers of the bank (outside of the 'selling list').

Workbooks are also provided at each level, in addition to the training. A sample outline of content for a basic sales agents' handbook is provided in Appendix C at the end of the chapter.

Recruiting and dismissals

Sales agent teams usually need to be built up fast to take advantage of opportunities. They also have relatively high turnover rates, especially in the beginning (10% minimum, 50% maximum per year should be expected). Because of these factors, a good recruiting process and well-planned dismissal procedures are of critical importance. Senior team leaders are usually responsible for these, although the support team and the bank's HR department both have important co-ordinating and technical roles to play. As mentioned earlier, senior team leaders should be able to handle 5–10 new hiring and up to five dismissals per month to ensure HR plans remain on track.

Recruiting process

The typical recruiting process is outlined in Figure 3.2.

Figure 3.2: Sales agent recruitment process

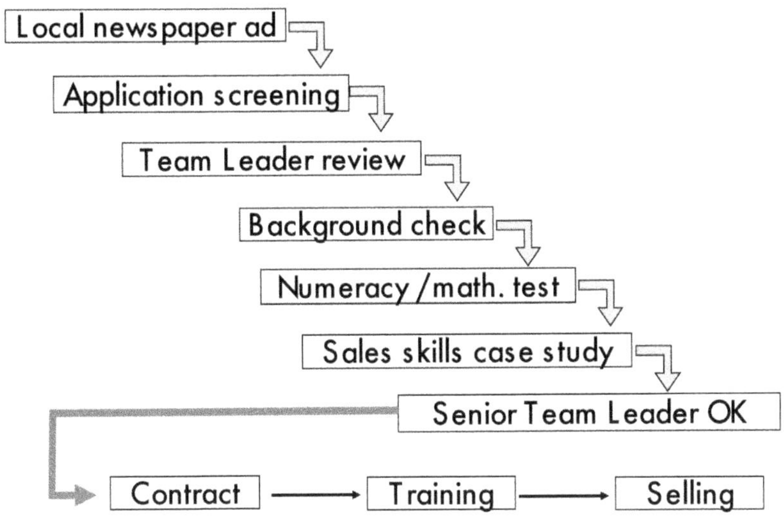

Source: 3-i Inc.

The following notes apply to the process:

- 'Application screening' should be outsourced if at all possible. It would otherwise create severe workload issues for team leaders because of the high volume of recruiting;
- 'Team leader review' is the first, screening, interview;
- 'Background check' should include verification of (lack of) a criminal record and previous employment;
- The mathematical test is mandatory;
- The sales skills test may use non-financial product sales situations. These can both put the applicant at ease and allow for checking pure sales skills, without having to allow for an understanding of financial products.

Success factors

The following have been found to correlate with the future success of newly hired sales agents, generally in this order:

- Numeracy, reliability, manners and appearance – these are 'knock-out' factors when comes to hiring. Nobody should be hired without being acceptable in these areas;
- Enthusiasm – self-motivation, ability to effectively plan own time, need to succeed;

- Financial services experience – note how this is contrary to the situation with branch agents, where financial services experience had a relatively low level of correlation with success;
- Sales skills;
- History of self-employment.

Age and gender have been found not to show any correlation with future success.

Dismissals

Sales agents who have breached their contract, or who have performed below minimum sales expectations for three consecutive months, should be dismissed. Dismissals should be recommended by the team leader and approved / initiated by the senior team leader. Terms of dismissal must be part of the contract. Note that minimum sales expectations should increase in time as agents gain more experience. While the three-month time limit may seem severe it should not be lengthened if one wishes to run an efficient sales agent network.

Contract

The contract should set out clearly all expectations for both sides. Contracts for agents, team leaders and senior team leaders differ slightly. Contracts for sales agents and leaders are much simpler than those for branch agents.

Generally, contracts should cover:

- Minimum sales expectations and remuneration structure;
- Restrictions on delegating work, signing in the bank's name, having relationships with other financial institutions;
- Expectations in terms of document verification, prospect targeting, dress, manner, attending training;
- Rules on credit, audit, service quality, expense management, taxes, etc;
- Benefits provided, beyond remuneration – for example, the bank's fleet rates for car leasing, employee loan rates as long as contract is valid, subsidised mobile phones, provision of business cards, etc;
- Disengagement clause and process, causes for termination.

A sample contract for sales agents is given in Appendix B, to help the reader construct his own – taking into account local business needs and legal / regulatory issues. Contracts for team leaders and senior leaders would of course include additional items such as personnel responsibility and responsibility for the results of their teams.

Remuneration

The same basic comments and questions apply as those discussed under remuneration for branch agents, in Chapter 2. However, because sales agents are at the individual sales staff level, the optimal design and the answer to the key questions posed previously all differ.

Upfront commissions should be used for sales agents, with no ongoing element as was the case with branch agents. Sales agents should be focused on achieving short-term objectives and should be rewarded for one-time product sales only.

Minimum sales expectations should be set (again, unlike the recommendation for branch agents). Sales expectations should be set in three different ways:

1. Minimum expectation, to qualify for the fixed part of the compensation the agent receives. If it is missed three months in a row the sales agent should face dismissal;
2. Hurdle rates to qualify for the variable part of their basic compensation;
3. Exceptional performance, above which bonuses or other rewards are given.

Sales need to be verified before remuneration is given (different from what is recommended for branch agents). Examples of 'real sales' are:

- Loans – funds have been disbursed (this, of course, assumes both credit approval and customer take-up of the offered credit);
- Deposit accounts – funds have been deposited into the account. In some cases account activity or longevity of funds may be required, for example if the business faces special challenges with inactive accounts or potential abuse by sales agents. The latter refers to the practice of opening several accounts for friends, putting funds in to qualify for commission, then quickly removing the funds and opening new accounts with them to earn extra commission;
- Credit cards – the physical card has been sent / picked up.

Ideally, the portfolios generated by sales agents would be tracked to uncover any systematic abuse which may not be obvious upfront. However, there is no need for tracking, for example, 90-day past due loan accounts (as was recommended for branch agents). Because sales agents have no authority to open accounts or approve credit, they should not be held strictly responsible for portfolio quality. It is the bank's responsibility to put in place the right reward structure and internal processes to drive portfolio development in the right direction.

Commission rates can be changed more frequently than in the case of branch agents. The structure of commission and contractual agreement with the agent should allow for this. Sales agents also respond well to tactical initiatives and sales promotions. There needs to be enough flexibility in the commission structure to accommodate these as well.

Knock-out criteria for sales agents are also simpler than for branch agents. Two general criteria usually suffice:

1. Following the rules as agreed in the contract;
2. Providing a good level of customer service, as verified by lack of complaints and regular check-up calls by team leaders and the support team to customers.

Starting up the commission system

As a rule of thumb, sales agents should receive 100% salary for the first three months.

From the fourth month, fixed compensation should drop to 25% and 75% should become variable. This 75% variable part would be earned by delivering 100% on sales expectation. It follows then that the variable part could grow to more than 75% if the agent qualifies for it with higher performance. There should be no cap on the variable part – the more the agent earns, the more profitable he is for the bank.

Both the compensation rates and sales expectations can change as time passes. Table 3.4 shows a recommended sales expectation schedule for new sales agents for the first six months.

Table 3.4: Sales schedule for new sales agents

Number of products to be sold, per month			
Month	Minimum expectation	Hurdle rate	Bonus performance
1	3	5	Not applicable
2	6	10	Not applicable
3	10	15	Not applicable
4	15	20	25
5	15	20	25
6	15	20	25

Source: 3-i Inc.

The 'hurdle rate' is more like 'expected average performance' for the first three months, because only a fixed salary is paid. That is, no extra money is earned if the agent delivers at the hurdle rate. However, it is useful to track the development of new agents against this benchmark.

Commission structures

Sales agent commissions

From the fourth month onward, fixed income should drop to 25% of the total, based on delivering 100% on expectations. A proven commission system is as follows:

- Base – earned if minimum expectations are met;
- Fees – earned on a per-product-sold basis, as long as the hurdle rate is achieved. The hurdle rate is equal to 100% sales expectations – the fee structure should take this into account;
- Bonus – earned for exceptional performance, meeting the bonus performance rate. Provides unlimited upside to the agent.

The structure of commission elements would be:

- Base is a simple draw / salary which should be no more than 25% of total compensation.

- Fees are upfront commissions paid per product sale. They can be structured in different ways – fixed, variable, mixed, capped, etc. The level of specific fees should be set based on reviewing the following key points:
  - Bank's needs and objectives;
  - Product profitability;
  - Competitive commission structures;
  - Cost of acquisition of new customer with same product through a different channel;
  - Regional variances – special business development focus in an area, easy versus difficult prospecting based on local wealth, population density or other factors;
  - Special promotions.
- Bonus is paid for exceptional sales performance. There are several variations on designing bonus schemes. The best motivational value is usually represented by a mixture of an ongoing 'basic bonus' structure and periodic 'special rewards'.
- Basic bonus means that extra income can be earned in each month as long as 'bonus performance' is achieved in that month. This can be provided by:
  - Progressive fees on extra product sales, e.g. a basic fee for the first 20 sales and a higher fee for each additional sale as long as there were at least 25 sales in the month;
  - Progressive 'booster' fees applying to all sales if bonus performance is achieved. For example, in the above case, the higher fees would be paid on all product sales once bonus performance is achieved, not only on the additional sales;
  - One-time payouts, triggered at certain levels. Again, using the above example, a special $X fee could be paid if 25 sales are achieved, another $Y if 30 are achieved.
- Special rewards should encourage ongoing strong, and growing, superior performance. There is a great variety of these rewards, both in terms of what to reward and how to reward it. For example, these can be given:
  - To top performers (as long as they also meet certain sales expectations);
  - Based on three or six months' results;
  - Based on delivering bonus performance for six consecutive months.

The rewards can be as simple as public recognition, or a dinner, trip, extra money and more.

Team leader / senior leader commissions

Team leaders and senior team leaders should participate in a similar remuneration structure, with some exceptions:

- Their base, fee and bonus payment levels and qualifying sales results are different;
- Their results should obviously include the sales of their teams;
- Senior team leaders do not engage in personal selling, so they do not get 'fees'. They should be base + bonus rewarded, at levels that elevates them above team leaders, all else being equal;
- Their other responsibilities should be taken into account in the reward structure. For example, HR stability is a good qualifying factor for senior team leaders to earn their bonus.

Financials

Financial modelling for the setting up of a sales agent network should be relatively straightforward. There is very little cost involved with the agents themselves and those that exist are both easy to estimate and easy to control (e.g. does the bank provide car subsidies or not, what is the cost of allowing them part-time use of a branch desk, etc). Most of the costs are in their compensation. Because at least 75% of that is strictly tied to product sales, it should create no issues as long as the compensation system is designed to make money for the bank.

As a general rule, 10–20% is the overhead part of the total cost of such a channel, while 80–90% is direct sales compensation. Products sold through the sales agent channel should result in new product sales (that is, not cross-selling but selling to new customers) at 15–50% of the comparable acquisition costs through other bank channels.

Implementation

It is important to start any implementation on a small scale, so that no overhead is built up before the new channel can support it and is proven as an ongoing proposition. At the same time, start-up must be fast.

Key proven first steps in setting up a sales agent channel are as follows:

1. Develop a business case, based on only a few, carefully selected products, to sell.
2. Set targets and operational objectives;
3. Employ a senior sales manager in charge of the network;
4. Employ two sales support staff, reporting to the above manager;
5. Prepare procedures, standards, systems, compensation plan, training;
6. Decide if three team leaders would be available from among employees, maybe on a temporary basis only;
7. Start recruitment to set up three teams of maximum six to eight agents in each (having three team leaders to start them up would speed up the process, hence point 6 above);

8. Monitor performance of teams for six months, review lessons learned, define changes needed before expanding;
9. Hire additional support staff based on expansion plan;
10. Start recruiting for expansion;
11. Full start-up.

Timing for the above should be:

- Steps 1 to 7: six months maximum;
- Steps 8 and 9: seven to eight months;
- Steps 10 and 11: three to four months, assuming 100–300 agents.

The total time is therefore 16–18 months. I would hope that this timing could be reduced to no more than 12 months, by using the information and templates presented in this chapter.

Summary

- Setting up a sales agent channel is a fast, flexible, cost-efficient way of improving customer acquisition capabilities.
- It provides faster and lower-cost customer acquisitions, but with a very narrow product range.
- It is a much simpler channel than branch agents and can be controlled with less effort.
- It is, however, no replacement for other, more traditional channels. It does not / should not provide services, cross-selling or a full product range.
- It is a very tactical, short-term, narrowly product sales-focused channel. It should only be used as an add-on, while maintaining all other channel capabilities.
- Because of its relative simplicity, control issues are not as great as with branch agents. However, the administrative burden can be high, due to high turnover.
- This chapter should have provided enough information for the practitioner to:
  - Evaluate the pros and cons of such a channel;
  - Plan how it could be implemented, including a business case;
  - Shorten the implementation period by up to 50%, based on the templated information provided.

Appendix A – Sample prospect contact rules for sales agents

1. The sales agent is not allowed to delegate any duties which arise from agent's agreement with the bank.
2. The sales agent must take care of his/her appropriate appearance.
3. The sales agent is only allowed to deal with prospects who comply with the following criteria:
   i. Minimal monthly income of €X net (€Y gross);
   ii. Secondary or higher education.
4. The sales agent must pay attention to signs which may indicate poor credit worthiness of the prospect. All such observations should be reported to the bank. The sales agent should not accept a prospect's credit application form if there is strong doubt regarding credit or trustworthiness.
5. In the case of forwarding credit applications from doubtful prospects, the sales agent should flag them with the agreed code to signal to the bank that extra diligence is warranted.
6. The sales agent is not allowed to charge fees to prospects for his or her activities.
7. All the data collected by the sales agent must be based on original and up-to-date documents.
8. The prospect must sign all the documents and application form in the sales agent's presence.
9. The sales agent must certify copies of documents on every page.
10. The sales agent must inform the prospect regarding all the consequences resulting from breaking off the contract.
11. The sales agent must call the client/prospect after 14 days from delivering prospect's application form and required documents. This is aimed at clarifying any doubts connected with client's documents, exploring additional sales opportunities and checking for service delivery on the part of the bank. If necessary, the sales agent should also remind the client to deposit the minimum funds into the account.
12. The sales agent is not allowed to undertake any marketing actions without the bank's written permission.

Appendix B – Sample sales agent contract

Agreement,

Signed in _______, on ______________ by:

1. Bank A, located at_______________ in ______________, registered as ___________, at

________________, hereafter referred to as 'the Bank', represented by:

1) Name, title
2) Name, title

and

2. ____________, private entrepreneur, VAT registration ______________, sole proprietorship registration

________________, residing at ____________________, hereafter referred to as 'the Bank Representative'.

§1

1. The Bank Representative, as part of his entrepreneurship, will act as the Bank's paid intermediary in signing agreements for the sale of products and delivery of services to individual customers. The Bank Representative acting as an intermediary will:
    1. Find customers and offer them banking products;
    2. Inform potential customers about the Bank's range of products and services;
    3. Collect and verify documents needed by the Bank;
    4. Deliver to the Bank all forms and documents related to the banking products, especially application forms;
    5. Carry out duties requested by the Bank, connected with acquisition of new customers, e.g. assistance in organising promotional stands.

2. The Bank Representative is not authorised to sign contracts on behalf of the Bank, grant credit or open accounts. In relations with customers and prospects the Bank Representative should use the authorisation which is attached to this Agreement (Attachment No.1) and comply with rules outlined in Attachment No.2.
3. The Bank Representative is obliged to perform duties specified in points 1 and 2 personally, and with due accuracy. Prior to concluding the first procedure, he should inform the Customer that he is acting as the Bank's intermediary in delivering banking services.
4. The Bank Representative is obliged to represent the Bank in an appropriate manner and adhere to a dress code appropriate for the nature of the occupation. A suit for men and a matching skirt and jacket for women are understood as adequate garments. The Bank Representative will cover the cost of his/her garments.

§2

1. The Bank Representative is obliged to carry out the Agreement as a part of his entrepreneurship. The Bank can demand appropriate documents confirming such entrepreneurship as well as criminal record clearance.
2. The Bank is not obliged to pay the personal income tax or social or medical insurance payable on the Bank Representative's income subject to this Agreement.

§3

1. The Bank will pay monthly salary, bonus and commission for the duties outlined in §1 pts.1 and 4, performed by the Bank Representative, in the amount specified in Attachment No.3.
2. The Bank may grant a special bonus to the Bank Representative, should it be justified by the Bank Representative's special achievements in performing duties outlined in the Agreement.
3. The Bank Representative is obliged to deliver at least X applications for opening a bank account every week.
4. The Bank Representative is not entitled to the commission or bonus specified in pt.1, if the Bank Representative signs contract with the Bank on his own behalf.
5. The Bank Representative has the right to place claims regarding the calculated commission within three working days of receiving the Statement about the commission amount, mentioned in §5 pt.4.

§4

1. The Bank Representative is obliged to take every possible measure in order to have the application forms completed correctly and with due accuracy, as well as to help customers complete the application forms accurately and truthfully.
2. The Bank Representative is obliged to obtain the potential customer's signature on the copy of a statement outlined in Attachment No.4.
3. The Bank Representative is obliged to stamp each application form with his own stamp, which should include the following codes given by the Bank: Agent Name and Unique Identifier Number.
4. The Bank Representative will assume responsibility for entering the Agent Name code incorrectly or illegibly.

§5

1. The Bank is obliged to pay monthly salary, commissions and bonuses outlined in §3 pt.1, after the end of each month, within 12 working days of the date of the bill/invoice, by a bank transfer to the account given by the Bank Representative, with regard to the exceptions specified in pt.4.
2. Should the Agreement be terminated before the end of a month, the Bank Representative is entitled to a pro rata monthly salary.
3. The Bank Representative authorises the Bank to prepare bills/invoices based on the reports from the Bank's system. Bills/invoices for each month will be prepared by the fourth working day of the following month. The Team Leader will deliver the bills/invoices to the Bank Representative by the sixth working day of the month. The Bank Representative will sign the bills/invoices without delay and return them to the Team Leader.
4. The Bank will deliver the Statement of the commission amount to the Bank Representative by the sixth working day of the month following the calculation month. The Bank is also obliged to inform the Bank Representative that the forecast number of signed contracts will be lower than the Bank Representative may have expected.

§6

1. The Bank is obliged to train the Bank Representative, especially in the field of bank secrecy, banking products and personal data protection. The cost of the training will be covered by the Bank, with the exception of pts.4 and 5.
2. The Bank Representative must participate in such trainings under penalty of termination of the Agreement.
3. The Bank will inform the Bank Representative of the time and place of the training.
4. Should the Bank Representative, who has been trained by the Bank or whose training costs have been covered by the Bank, terminate the Agreement, the Bank Representative will refund documented costs of the training covered by the Bank, with the exception of pt.6. If the training is carried out by the Bank, the costs of training will include:
   a) Return travel costs;
   b) Accommodation and food;
   c) Training materials;
   d) Room rental (proportionally to number of participants).

   The maximum quarterly cost of trainings will not exceed € ____.
5. Should the Bank Representative, who has been trained by the Bank or whose training costs have been covered by the Bank, violate the provisions of §1, §6 or §7 of this Agreement, the Bank Representative will refund documented costs of the training covered by the Bank, with the exception of pt.6.
6. If the Bank Representative has provided agency services for at minimum six months after the end of the training or should the Bank give the Bank Representative notice of the Agreement's termination, the Bank Representative will be exempt from refunding the training costs specified in pt.4.

§7

1. The Bank Representative must not undertake any duties for other banks or financial institutions within the time of the Agreement's duration period.
2. Should the Bank Representative violate the rule of exclusivity specified in pt.1, the Bank may terminate the Agreement without notice.

§8

1. Under penalty of termination of the Agreement without notice, the Bank Representative:
    1) Will comply with the bank secrecy laws regulated by the Banking Law of_____________;
    2) Will comply with the personal data protection laws regulated by Personal Data Protection Act of _____________________________;
    3) Will comply with internal Bank regulations provided to the Bank Representative by the Bank;
    4) Must not sign contracts on the behalf of the Bank nor transgress in any other way the range of the Bank's authorisation.
2. Should the Bank be made responsible for a damage done by the Bank Representative as a result of his failure to comply with the regulations mentioned in pt.1, the Bank Representative will be subject to full liability for the damage and its mending. Should the Bank pay compensation for the damage, the Bank Representative will refund the compensation to the Bank, by paying the amount of the compensation, increased by the accrued interest from the day of payment of the compensation by the Bank to the day of refunding the compensation by the Bank Representative.
3. Termination of the Agreement, without the specified notice period, is tantamount to withdrawal of the authorisation to act as Bank's agent in signing contracts for providing banking services. In such case the Bank Representative is obliged to return the authorisation document to the Bank without any delay.

§9

1. The Agreement is signed for an indefinite period of time.
2. The Agreement may be terminated with a month's notice in the first year of its duration, two months' notice in the second year of its duration, and three months' notice in the third and subsequent years of its duration.
3. Should the Bank Representative fail to perform duties outlined in §1, §3 pt.3, §7 and §8 or should extraordinary circumstances occur, the Bank may terminate the Agreement without notice.
4. Should the Bank be in arrears with payment of salary, commission or bonus specified in Attachment No.3, for two calendar months, or should extraordinary circumstances occur, the Senior Team Leader may terminate the Agreement without notice.
5. The Bank Representative is obliged to deliver to the Bank a Statement outlined in Attachment No.5 along with Statements of the customers mentioned in §4 pt.2 before termination of the Agreement.
6. Should the Bank Representative fail to submit the Statement in the manner outlined in pt.5, both parties assume that no potential customer has proposed the Bank Representative to sign a contract before the termination of the Agreement.

§10

Both parties agree that all letters related to the subject of this Agreement sent to the Bank Representative's address as specified in the Agreement are effectively delivered.

§11

All issues not regulated by this Agreement are subject to Agency agreement provisions of the Civil Code.

§12

Any disputes will be settled by the ______ Banks Association's Court of Arbitration, subject to its internal regulations.

§13

The Agreement becomes binding as of signing by both parties.

§ 14

Any changes to this Agreement in order to be valid need to be made in written format.

§15

The Agreement consists of two identical copies, one for each of the parties.

______________________________ Bank Representative

______________________________ Bank

Attachment No.1

Authorisation

Place, date

Bank A, based in __________________________ authorises ____________________, the Bank Representative, to act as the Bank's intermediary in signing agreements regarding providing banking services of Bank A (without the right to sign contracts on the Bank's behalf or accept cash).

/signatures/

Attachment No.2

Sales agent prospect contact rules

(Same as described under Appendix A earlier)

Attachment No.3

Detailed conditions of Bank Representative's salary, commission and bonus payment

I. Monthly salary:

a) The monthly salary amounts to € ______;

b) The monthly salary will be paid to the Bank Representative under the condition that the Bank Representative has finalised at least X bank account and/or credit contracts, subject to commission payable monthly.

II. Contracts subject to commission:

1) Deposit account:

a) €XX for each deposit account contract signed by the Bank through the Bank Representative in a given month, with the exceptions of pts.b–d;

b) The commission will not be paid if the minimum first payment made by the customer (total amount paid on the day of first payment) is lower than €YY;

c) The commission will not be paid if the customer fails to make the first payment in 92 days of signing the contract;

d) If the Bank Representative finalises more than one deposit account contract signed by the Bank with one customer, the commission will be paid only for the first contract.

2) Current account – standard type:

€ZZ for each current account (standard type) contract signed by the Bank through the Bank Representative, if the minimum first payment (total amount paid in the first day) is made by the customer within 92 days of signing the contract and is not lower than €___.

3) Current account – active type:

€______ for each current account with extended limit (active type) contract signed by the Bank through the Bank Representative, if the minimum first payment (total amount paid on the day of first payment) is made by the customer within 92 days of signing the contract and is not lower than the monthly amount of transfers into the account declared by the customer. If the customer had not declared any specific amount of transfers into the account, the minimum amount should not be lower than €_____.

4) Consumer credit:

1 % of the credit volume granted and disbursed by the customer within a calendar month, on the basis of the consumer credit contract signed by the Bank through the Bank Representative in each calendar month.

5) MasterCard Basic credit card:

€____ for each MasterCard Basic credit card contract signed by the Bank through the Bank Representative. The date of placing order for the credit card in the Bank's system is regarded by the Bank as the issue date, serving as the basis for the commission payment.

6) MasterCard Gold credit card:

€_____ for each MasterCard Gold credit card contract signed by the Bank through the Bank Representative. The date of placing order for the credit card in the Bank's system is regarded by the Bank as the issue date, serving as the basis for the commission payment.

III. Bonus for the number of bank account and/or credit contracts, subject to commission:

€_____ for every 14 bank account and/or credit contracts signed by the Bank through the Bank Representative, subject to commission in a calendar month.

Attachment No.4

Customer's statement

Place, date

I,

Name:

Surname:

Permanent address:

confirm that the Bank Representative:

Name:

Surname:

Agent name

is negotiating with me signing [enter product name] contract/contracts with Bank A. The above statement does not create for either party any obligation to sign the contract.

____
Customer

Attachment No. 5

Statement

Place, date

I, [enter name and surname of the Agent], confirm that as of [enter date], I am negotiating signing current account and/or credit contracts by the Bank and/or am engaged in preparation of documents necessary to sign current account and/or credit contracts with the following potential customers:

Name	Surname	Permanent address	Contract

I will deliver all documents related to the above customers to the Bank before termination of the Agreement, i.e. [enter date closing the notice period]. I will not undertake any actions in order to obtain customers for the Bank after termination of the Agreement.

Bank Representative

Appendix C – Sample list of content for sales agents' handbook

First impressions:

- Dress code, appearance;
- Professional behaviour.

Work process:

- Call (cold, warm);
- Meeting (arranging, conducting);
- Obtaining applications;
- Verifying documents and information;
- Submitting applications;
- Follow-up.

Prospecting:

- Sources of information;
- Cold and warm calling;
- Preparing for personal meeting.

Developing and executing own promotions:

- Allowed and prohibited activities;
- Calculating payback;
- Defining offers;
- Support materials;
- Getting approval from the bank.

Prospecting calls – all with sample scripts:

- Cold calls;
- Warm calls;
- Standard prospecting calls;
- Calls based on own promotion;
- Calls supporting central promotions;
- Follow-up calls to contacts initiated by other channels.

Personal meeting:

- Process, time scale, location;
- Appearance, behaviour;

- Focused product sale;
- Identifying additional needs;
- Objection handling;
- Closure techniques;
- Recap of meeting;
- Asking for referrals.

Meeting follow-up:

- Evaluating, learning, changing;
- Tracking conversion efficiencies:
    - Call to contact;
    - Contact to meeting;
    - Meeting to application (for product or offer);
    - Application to sale;
- Follow-up call, points to cover.

Handling objections:

- List of most common objections and best replies.

Work plan:

- Goal setting;
- Time management;
- Activity planning: monthly, weekly, daily;
- Staying on track, changing plans;
- Benchmarking.

Administrative issues:

- Allowed and disallowed activities;
- Submitting applications;
- Expense management;
- Legal and regulatory items;
- Other.

Chapter 4
Intermediary channels: maximising third-party relationships

Introduction

Intermediaries can provide crucial support: fast, flexible, low-cost market coverage, with face-to-face service to customers and expert support for the bank's products. As such, many banks use several different types of intermediaries, from independent brokerage networks to joint venture sales finance operations. This chapter deals with some of the more specific and practical issues of setting up and managing such networks.

Basic principles

The following principles have been used successfully by many financial institutions in making evaluations of alliance opportunities:

- Potential alliance partners to be considered should be:
  - For profit organisations;
  - Organisations with goals, strategies and profile close to the bank's;
  - If non-profit organisations, then without an advocacy stand.
- Unless otherwise clearly articulated in the bank's strategy, alliance offers should be branded under the bank's name or should be co-branded (but not 'white label' offers).
- The bank must own the customer's financial relationship. This is often a breaking point in negotiations with third-party, 'sales force for hire' outfits, which would normally want to control the relationship with customers they acquired for the bank. This must not be allowed to happen.
- High-level and high-quality support for the development and implementation of the deal should be assured by the potential alliance partner.
- To proceed with any deal, it first must satisfy three conditions:
  - It must be on strategy for the bank;
  - It must pay back within the financial hurdle rates imposed by the bank;
  - There must be factual evidence to support the assumption that the alliance would succeed – research, market experience or similar.
- Payback needs to be calculated based on acquisition costs saved (e.g. media, sales commission) to bring in the same number and same quality of customers as assumed by the business case.
- One-to-one or semi-exclusive negotiations should be guaranteed.
- Only exclusive deals should be considered. Exceptions to this rule must be justified case-by-case, by a strong business case and a long-term strategic overview to ensure no negative effects later.

An alliance opportunity only makes sense if it creates a win/win/win for all parties involved: the bank, its alliance partner, the consumer. For market-wide deals, consumer research is essential to ensure this. At the local level, personal investigations by the district manager or branch manager may be all that can be done.

Two examples follow that highlight the importance of research / investigations.

Case study 6: Example 1 – North America

A mid-sized bank wanted to focus on real estate agents (REAs) as intermediaries to promote its mortgage offer during a real estate market downturn. Straight promotions targeting the REA community quickly fizzled out. Research revealed that agents felt uncomfortable getting extra benefits (on top of their commission from the bank) when their customers got nothing extra. They felt the bank was possibly taking money out of what it could have offered to the customer and using it to subsidise gifts to the agents.

In response, a new mortgage product which offered a lower initial interest rate in return for an upfront lump-sum payment was repackaged and repositioned as follows. For home sellers, it was positioned as a way to avoid having to cut the resale price in a tough market. For a smaller sum they could offer a low-rate mortgage to go with the property to entice buyers turned off by high rates. For the home buyer, it was communicated as a very special offer. Not only a lower rate (thanks to the seller), but also a very flexible product (thanks to the bank) and a great opportunity (available thanks to the REA who negotiated the deal with the bank and the seller). For the REA, it was presented as a way to sell homes faster, therefore generating more commission income in a slow market. But it was also pointed out how their customers (sellers and buyers) benefited and how this benefit was linked to the agent personally in the bank's promotional materials.

The results were outstanding as all involved parties felt they had a win. It would not have happened without the research that went into developing the right approach to the alliance with REAs.

Case study 7: Example 2 – Europe

Another mid-sized bank started to develop consumer finance deals, but at the local level. Branches were encouraged to build alliances with local retailers, especially small but growing ones that may have been previously ignored. Branch people soon faced the issue that wherever they presented their offer the retailer quickly learned it was a good deal. However, having been educated by the bank in this area, retailers went 'shopping' around the competition to get competing offers, to give their customers a choice of different financing offers. This cut the potential business gain dramatically.

Not having access to research, a branch manager and his sales development officer studied the dynamics of competing consumer finance offers and their impact on retailers. What they found was very interesting. Strong anecdotal evidence suggested that rather than increasing sales, competing financing offers actually decreased sales at retailers.

The reasons were as follows: sales staff working the floor in, say, a hardware store are not trained in financing offers. So when the customer asks them "Which of these two financing offers is better?" they cannot answer. The customer is confused and worried that he may pick the wrong bank. But, having understood that good financing is available, he will also no longer pay cash. So he walks away to think it over, without buying anything. And in many cases never comes back...

Armed with this information, local sales people developed their business penetration strategy, stressing the benefits of single source financing to retailers and locking up deals fast.

Contracts – overview

When structuring an alliance deal the following key areas should be addressed:

- Access to each other's customer bases for cross-selling.
- Use of each other's sales and service channels to do the same and ensure after-sales service in the best possible way.
- Developing products or product features for each other.
- Engaging in joint product development to address new opportunities.
- Engaging in joint business development.
- Clarifying and agreeing expectations towards each other:
  - During the development phase – timing, quality;
  - During the co-operation phase – sales results, service levels.
- Disengagement:
  - How can the contract be annulled;
  - Who keeps what part of the customer relationships jointly developed;
  - What are the follow-up customer contact rules – e.g. no competitive offer directed at the jointly gained customers from another bank for 24 months following termination of the contract, etc.

Note that not all of the above areas are applicable with all partnerships. The areas are provided as a checklist, to ensure nothing gets overlooked.

Third-party types

There are so many potential third-party relationships a retail bank can set up that it is easy to get lost in details. It is therefore useful to immediately sort out the potential partnerships into main categories and sub-divide those further as needed. A potential division / sub-division model is given below.

Financial intermediaries

Banks – A bank may decide, for example, that it does not wish to set up its own credit capabilities. Granting retail loans requires statistical modelling, credit scoring, extra verification processes, collection, potential securitisation, etc. A bank with a strong focus on high net worth individuals (HNWIs) with investment needs may want to avoid the cost and effort needed to build its own credit facilities. Yet, to serve the full range of its customers' needs it has to be able to provide access to credit. It therefore may look for outside providers.

Insurance companies – Insurance companies involved in other relationships may want to 'recruit' a bank if the other partner's customers need credit. In return, the insurance provider may ask for an exclusive deal for providing credit insurance on all such loans granted. Insurance companies also have cash management and other banking-related needs for their customers. On the other hand, they may have large customer bases to cross-sell to, and a well-trained sales force to sell the bank's products for extra commission.

Other financial services companies – One example could be a company focusing on pension investments and realising that its target customers need accounts to transfer funds or credit to make an early investment purchase.

Broker networks: independent or majority owned – These can be with street presence or have an outreach agent force only. They can be independent or owned by a majority shareholder, usually a financial institution. They offer a range of products (even the majority owned ones!) to their customers, from different providers. Sometimes they can also be broken down further, based on their size and set-up:

- Large – large, independent brands, usually with regional or national presence;
- Small – small, local presence only, with a few outlets or agents;
- Pooled – a collection of smaller brokerages may come together under an umbrella brand for better economies of scale. (In these cases the bank must make sure that it can negotiate at the HQ level and keep in mind that a longer set-up process is needed. The deal usually has to be 'sold' to the independent members to get the support needed.)

Retailers – point-of-sale (POS) sales finance

Hypermarkets and supermarkets – These stores sell a wide variety of goods in addition to foodstuffs. Examples include Tesco, Cora, Auchan or Wal-Mart. They draw a large number of shoppers, many of whom need an 'on the spot' loan to be able to buy larger-ticket items such as a TV.

White goods / electronics – Retailers specialising in selling home electronics, PCs, white goods (washing machines, refrigerators and other home appliances). Normally about 10% of their sales require financing.

Brown goods – Furniture and related goods. Again, these are mostly large-ticket items, needing sales finance offers. Brown goods retailers present their own unique challenges due to long lead times between purchase decision and taking ownership of the goods. These will be discussed later.

Automobile – A classic partnership set-up, where bank loans are needed to facilitate the sales.

Other (DIY, drugstores, etc) – Retailers with large ticket items and/or large customer bases present good opportunities. For those with large customer bases but lower-ticket items different approaches are needed. Credit (POS finance) opportunities are limited but a large base may present good credit card sales opportunities, especially on a co-branded basis.

Other

Utilities, telcos – Funds transfer offers are the starting points with these types of alliances, but credit cards and small personal loans can be good follow-up opportunities.

Government – Different levels of governments collect and disburse funds for different reasons. Governments are usually motivated to outsource funds handling to banks to cut costs and force suspect cash payments out of the system.

Travel services – Beyond the obvious insurance and credit card needs, 'save up' offers and other innovative products may be distributed through travel agents.

Real estate – A home is usually the largest purchase people make, coupled with the largest financial liability – a mortgage loan. Estate agents are motivated to pre-qualify their buyers to ensure they present homes within their affordability range. They are therefore usually very positive towards offering assistance with mortgages (with the help of a bank provider) to their customers.

Direct sellers – Catalogue retailers, PC direct sellers, other mail order companies.

Others – From airlines to plastic surgery clinics, the possibilities are wide ranging.

Benefits

Some of the key benefits of an intermediary set-up are as follows:

1. *Lower cost of acquisition.* Because the partner either already has a relationship with the customer, or is generating a large volume of prospects through its own offers, a lot of the upfront marketing costs can be saved. Expressed as TOC (take-on cost), POS acquisitions cost 3–4% and broker acquisitions cost 5–8% when a traditional, advertising-driven campaign would cost 10–20%.
2. *'Guaranteed' flow of new balances.* Based on the track record of the intermediaries (banks, brokers, retailers) it can be fairly accurately calculated how much business one would generate. For example, with white / brown goods retailers 10% of their total sales (turnover) is financed. It can therefore be assumed that 2% of their T/O (turnover) will turn into POS loan balances in Year 1, rising to 5% in Year 2 and 10% by Year 3.
3. *High-quality personal service.* Many people still resist remote sales and want to talk to someone face-to-face. Brokers, qualified supermarket staff and trained estate agents can all accomplish this.
4. *Fast, flexible presence.* Because we do not need to build real estate for personal presence, we can penetrate new regions much faster using third-party alliances. At the same time, if we need to withdraw, it can be done without having to worry about disposing of both real assets and people.
5. *Work sharing.* By having, for example, supermarket personnel do loans pre-qualifications or gather signatures / papers required for new accounts, a portion of the branch staff's work can be outsourced, while remaining within regulatory limits. (Note: As regulations vary a great deal between countries, this point definitely needs to be verified through local legal advice!)

6. *Information for later cross-selling.* Servicing utility or telco accounts provides a wealth of information about people's spending habits and what they can afford. This will allow the bank to tailor specific sales offers to selected segments, with high efficiency.
7. *Organisational experience.* Just as having one's own direct sales agent (DSA) sales force should be a precursor to engaging in broker relationships, having broker relationships should be a precursor to building one's own branch agent network. This is because each step along this line represents an increasing level of risk, but builds on experienced gained from the previous step and provides a knowledge platform for the next.

Having listed the benefits to us, make sure to always keep in mind the benefits that incur to our third-party partners. USPs (unique selling propositions) will be covered later. The following are some basic benefits, which incur whether or not we put that little extra behind our offer.

Benefits to partners

1. *Increased customer loyalty.* For brokers, this is because they have an additional (good) offer that will demonstrate to their customers the broker has their best interests in mind. For retailers, this is a research-proven fact, relying on the effect of not losing customers to the competition when the customer is ready to make a large purchase but lacks immediate funds.
2. *Higher in-store spend for retailers.* Studies show an average of 10% additional sales if POS finance offers are available. Results are pretty much the same across hypermarkets, brown and white goods.
3. *Better customer information.* This is what drove a number of industries, such as airlines, to enter into banking alliances in the first place. Airlines, for example, used to track passenger miles and other efficiency measures but not the personal habits of their flyers (with the rare exception of some frequent-flyer programmes). Being able to identify individual patterns among their customers is therefore of great importance to them. Banks must track credit card activities at the individual level and can, within privacy confines, help airlines identify patterns important to their business. The same holds true for retailers, who increasingly look at information from their POS finance partners as value added.

Additional, inherent, benefits are detailed earlier under 'Third-party types'.

Watch-outs

Most benefits come with strings attached. This section reviews some of the areas that require careful attention in the management of third-party alliances, to make sure our costs do not end up outweighing the benefits.

1 *Beware of full business dynamics.* While TOCs might be lower, so might be margins and average ticket sizes. A full business case must always be done to understand profit dynamics. For example, in many markets 'Pay nothing for

six months!' or '0% interest for six months!' offers dominate the POS finance world. One can imagine what this does to interest margins...

2 *Beware of full business dynamics – again.* Loan sizes, for example, will vary by channel. The following comparison is taken from a real market of mid-level personal lending development in Europe:

Channel and credit type	€ / new credit booked
Direct sourced personal term loan	1,800
Broker sourced personal term loan	2,000
POS sourced personal term loan	600
POS sales finance loan	300

Combined with point 1, this should caution anyone about relying on POS sales finance loans to drive immediate revenues in this given market.

3 *Ride on your strengths.* It is easy to forget about operational costs when doing an aggressive sales push for new business. But if our operational capabilities are not excellent, then getting a lot of heavily transaction-oriented accounts may not make sense, even if acquisition costs are low and balances acceptable.

Case study 8: Operational cost problems

My most relevant personal experience in this area comes from a business review that showed cross-sell costs in a market were three times higher than acquisition costs. This should not be so. Cross-sell costs are almost always lower than upfront acquisition expenses. It turned out that the subsidiary in the given market aggressively acquired 'salary accounts' of state employees, driven by good relationships with different levels of governments.

The first problem was that the operational costs for these accounts were high and most employees took their full balances out at the branches within a few days. This left nothing to make money on.

The second problem was that the subsidiary could not effectively cross-sell to the account holders thus acquired. Hence, profitability remained elusive.

The third crucial problem was that the low upfront acquisition cost (of unprofitable accounts) presented a picture of efficiency for sales and marketing that masked the overall negative situation. Hence, no steps were taken to address it.

Following the business review the situation was turned around. Fees were introduced for salary accounts to cover costs and waived when profitable cross-selling occurred. This drove an efficient cross-sell focus that managed to fix the profit issue.

4 *Risks to the Brand.* Brand dilution is one risk, as a bank provides white label offers instead of building its own brand. Reputational risk is another, as any potential negative publicity for an intermediary may also taint its key partners. As these are essentially marketing-related items, they will not be detailed further here.

5 *Fraud.* Dealing through third parties always increases the risk of fraud. Good preventative measures, backed up by strong IT / operational platforms and strong audit processes need to be in place to mitigate them. (See also references to related items in Chapter 2 and Chapter 3.)

6 *Understand industry dynamics and the risks they represent.* A good example of this point is brown goods POS sales finance. In many parts of Europe it may take up to eight weeks to deliver furniture selected and ordered in store. While the customer needs to take credit immediately to buy the goods, he will not receive them until much later. This creates not only legal issues of responsibility (who is responsible if the goods arrive damaged? can the customer stop payment? has the money taken as a loan already been paid?) but financial ones as well. For example, when should the bank pay the retailer? When should the customer start paying the bank? Who is making a margin, and when? While the questions may seem trivial, they could easily create a level of complexity making it prohibitive for a bank to engage in this kind of POS sales activity.

Structures

There are three basic types of third-party deal structures for financial services providers. There is also a further type which sometimes gets confused with real third-party deals. This is when a non-bank entity owns a company with a banking licence (however limited it may be) and uses its offers, targeting its own customers with it.

An example is Banque Accord, owned by the Auchan supermarket chain. Because Auchan offers POS financing and other financial products from Banque Accord, many believe this is a third-party relationship. In fact, it is not, because the intermediary (Auchan) controls the provider (Accord) instead of having a partnership agreement with it. This point needs to be mentioned upfront to avoid confusion and explain why this type of set-ups is not covered in this section.

The three true intermediary type relationships are as follows:

1. Joint ventures;
2. Revenue / cost / profit share;
3. Straight commission system.

Joint ventures

Prime examples are the Tesco Personal Finance model in the UK and Europe (Tesco / Royal Bank of Scotland), or President's Choice Bank in Canada (Loblaws / Canadian Imperial Bank of Commerce). These models are based on a split ownership of a joint venture which will then facilitate the provision of financial services from the banking partner through to the customers of the distribution partner.

They would normally focus on the longer term, with clear definitions of sharing costs, efforts, management roles, revenues and profits. On average, it takes about three years to reach break even and four years to reach payback for either party. This compares favourably with branch paybacks.

These types of set-ups are recommended for longer-term, strategic relationships only. Governance and (in the case of international ambitions) matching international geographic coverage are key. Sadly, both Tesco Personal Finance and President's Choice Bank have hit rough patches lately. It appears that no such model will survive in the longer term, due to conflicting interests which are glossed over by 'strategic co-operation' ideals – but cannot withstand the daily reality of profit pressure.

The basic idea is that the participating partners set up a joint venture (JV), ideally 50/50 owned, with joint management. The banking partner would provide financial products (including coverage for operational, credit loss, and certain sales support costs) while the retail partner would donate floor space in their outlets, full access to their customer base and dedicated referral / sales activities.

The JV runs a 'shadow profit and loss (P/L)' ledger and splits the net profit remaining at the end. It is easy to see at least two emerging issues:

- No profit for the first few years. This may not be a big issue if the two parties agree on causes and steps to remedy the situation. If that is not the case, then mutual blame can easily set in, putting strain on the arrangement.
- Unequal geographic coverage. If both parties move cross-border, but not into the same markets, tensions will follow. Why should the party that established itself in a new market at its own expense still split net profit with the one that did not follow?

Revenue / cost / profit share

This set-up attempts to strike a compromise between the strategic JV approach and the more tactical straight commission-based one. In this case, the two parties set out a system whereby they would share costs, responsibilities, liabilities, revenues and, hence, profits at the end. However, there is no joint ownership, no joint management.

Depending on the agreements, there may also be a commission element built in for either party. For example, a hypermarket's own sales staff may be incentivised for sales referred or booked, while the POS finance provider may get a 'reverse commission' if it boosts the hypermarket's white goods sales with attractive financial offers.

Even with commission elements mixed in, this is a much 'cleaner' arrangement than the full JV approach and is indeed the fall-back position that many partners look at for long-term co-operation.

Straight commission system

The cleanest, easiest, but also most short-term set-up. The provider (the bank) offers a commission to the reseller (the third-party intermediary) on each verified sales. While it does not have a long-term arrangement locked in, it is a very clean starting point and offers the potential to turn into something more lasting based on proven results.

Compensation

At the heart of most agreements is the compensation structure. Note that most of the issues highlighted under DSA and branch agent compensation systems would also apply here. What follows is a practical review of some of the specific, third-party intermediary-based compensation structures.

First, it needs to be decided if compensation is based on new sales or portfolio accumulated. Second, any incentives on top of the basic compensation payments need to be designed. Third, the way the compensation is provided needs to be agreed: is it a flat amount or is it (almost) totally up to the intermediary, based on what price it charges for the offers it passes through? Finally, other types of compensation need to be agreed – beyond the standard 'volume-based' ones.

New sales versus portfolio

This essentially means whether the bank will pay commission based on the most recent new sales (incremental gains in the portfolio) or based on the total portfolio brought in so far by the given intermediary. The rule of thumb here is to always go for the 'new sales' approach. Opting for the 'portfolio' approach creates unforeseen future liabilities and complications, e.g. what happens when the contract is cancelled, should commission still be payable, can the bank 'repatriate' its own customers, etc. The portfolio approach also creates a guaranteed steady cashflow to the subsidiary and thus may not incentivise them for further hard work to develop the business.

Commission plus incentives

Commissions can be given based on flat fee, volumes, or any other combination. (See Chapter 2 and Chapter 3 for more detail.) On top of commissions, other incentives can be layered in. They should drive the right behaviour by the intermediaries' sales people. Commonly used incentives reward sales staff for:

- Credit quality;
- Number of cross-sales or referrals;
- Volume targets achieved or average ticket sizes;
- Auxiliary products (e.g. insurance covers) cross-sold;
- Audit scores;
- Service quality results;
- Term of deposits or loans.

Floor price approach

One way of combining several incentives into one is to offer a 'selling price', or floor-price, to the intermediaries for the different products. The bank can say: "At this amount, for this term, for this loan I would charge X% rate, and for this deposit I would give Y% interest." It is then up to the intermediary to generate its own reward by setting the 'resale' rates appropriately. This is very similar to what happens in the wholesale / retail sale domain. Retailers buy at the wholesale rate then set their own prices for reselling.

The advantages of this approach are simplicity and flexibility. Simplicity, because the bank can simply provide a pricing structure and forget about other variations. Flexibility, because it gives the intermediary the option of running its own 'loss leader' promotions, set regional prices, put its own incentive schedule into action (and take the cost of it from its own spread).

The drawback is that pricing control is given up by the bank. It may therefore be beneficial to set certain floor/ceiling prices, below/above which intermediaries cannot go. Otherwise the bank can easily undermine the success of its other distribution channels that lack the same flexibility.

Other support

Spending support or technical assistance may also be offered on several fronts from the bank to the intermediary. These could include, for example:

- Marketing spending support;
- Sales promotion materials;
- Training for sales staff…

… and more. A good contract would cover the scope, duration and qualifying criteria for all these support.

USPs

When selling through third-party intermediaries two sets of USPs (unique selling propositions) need to be considered. It is not enough to provide benefits for the end-customer; there must be benefits for the intermediary too. In addition, the two sets of benefits must mesh with each other.

Let us look at an example how these different USPs can be combined if a bank wishes to offer its credit products directly to customers, through brokers and through retail alliances. The items are from a real situation, from my own experience.

USPs for end-customers

These could focus on product benefits and convenience. For example:

- Flexible product design – allowing for overpayments, earning the right to use up the pre-paid periods by missing payments during periods of cash shortage (e.g. at Christmas);

- Flexible product set-up – tailoring the loan set-up to the individuals' needs, e.g. allowing the customer to pick the amount to pay and setting the term of the loan to achieve that – even if the term is 'odd', such as 27 months;
- On-the-phone pre-approval in 15 minutes.

USPs for intermediaries

These would include the above product benefits, presented as a route to more sales and, hence, profits and commissions. In addition, by providing a better service to customers, the intermediaries' image improves and customer loyalty should also increase. In addition, there are:

- Own-branded broker offers – allowing the broker to sell the above unique products under its own name, building a strong brand position;
- Own-branded loyalty payment card for retailers – allowing them to link loyalty offers and product-specific discounts to the cards, plus tracking customer information for better customer relationship management (CRM).

Additional USP for both

- Regional bank branding – building community appeal among both end-customers and local brokers by offering services from 'Bank A of Region X', instead of a far-removed bank from the capital city.

Note that pricing does not appear anywhere among the USPs. Offering differential pricing among different channels is dangerous and not recommended. The customer should decide based on the best value proposition for him by the different channels (phone, branch, broker, other) and make his choice based on that. Incentivising him to go to a broker by offering better price through that channel would quickly destroy profit on products sold through that channel (remember: we still have to pay the broker too!). On the other hand, offering a better price if the customer deals directly with the bank would alienate the brokers and other partners.

Rather, it is both product benefits (e.g. flexible product design) and process benefits (e.g. flexible product set-up) that are emphasised. Process benefits should be preferred over product benefits. They are more difficult for the competition to duplicate and present just as tangible a benefit as the best designed product features (which are also easier to copy).

Physical and process designs

Physical set-ups and integration

The one type of intermediary set-up that requires special attention here is the retail alliance partner type. Brokers have their own set-ups and other alliance partners vary so widely in their requirements that it is difficult to review templates or recommend approaches to follow.

Retail POS finance

There are several approaches to this. The first key differentiator is whether there is a physical presence for the bank in the retail outlet or not. It is always recommended that an on-site physical presence be established. This can either be in the store itself, or in an adjacent area.

For example, Tesco in Central Europe has credit desks near its electronics and home appliances areas, offering credit from Tesco Personal Finance but staffed by sales people from the banking partner. IKEA has an office for its banking partner past the cashiers but within its store or nearby in the mall. They are branded to the banking partner (e.g. Cetelem Credit Office) and staffed by bank employees.

In many other cases (e.g. Tesco UK) there is no physical presence in the stores, only brand presence. The store acts merely as a referral arena and, in some cases, as a place where documents can be signed, witnessed and gathered.

An in-between solution is when POS consumer credit is handled in one of the store's departments (usually at the customer service desk) by the store's own employees, passing on the request electronically to the bank and waiting for an on-the-spot response.

Process design

Process design should cover not only the sales process, but related services and operational processes too. There are many complicated-looking charts available which lay out, step by step, how the best processes should work. Their ultimate shape is governed by the specific circumstances, IT and operational limitations. It is therefore difficult to present ready-made templates. Instead, let us look at a simple overview of key steps in different parts of the design map.

We will use as an example a product that is widely sold and has some complications – personal loans. We will look at not only how the different steps play out (e.g. applications, approval, disbursement, repayment) but how they differ through different intermediary channels. In a simplistic way, let us imagine that we try to explain to someone how we imagine handling a new business set-up in a new country, selling loans through different channels but without our own branch or ATM network.

The review that follows is another real-life example, from my own experience.

Sales generation

- Loan applications are generated by above-the-line (ATL) and below-the-line (BTL) marketing, at broker outlets, retail and other partnerships, by sales agents and (eventually) at credit kiosk franchise outlets. ATL/BTL-generated applications are captured at website and call centre and followed up by the call centre or direct sales agents.
- Pre-qualification of applicants should be possible at each contact point. Sales agents need online access for on-the-spot credit reviews.

- Standard best practice is 15 minutes to 'yes', 1–2 days to cash, with a 60–80% approval rate.
- Fully remote processing must be possible if allowed by local regulations (e.g. if there is no need for signing anything in front of a bank employee).

Direct sourcing

- Application filled out online.
- Instant feedback provided on creditworthiness, based on information provided.
- Form is printed by applicant, original documents or copies attached as required by law (and given on the website), everything is mailed to the bank.
- Documents are verified, request approved or rejected, applicant notified (by call centre and by mail if requested).
- Funds are disbursed (if loan approved).

Broker sourcing

- Applicant discusses options with broker.
- Broker gathers information, inputs into the bank's pre-approval system, gets instant feedback based on information provided.
- Broker gathers documents and copies, fills out form, applicant signs, broker sends package to the bank.
- Documents are verified, application approved / rejected, funds disbursed (or not), the bank notifies broker first, then applicant.

Retailer sourcing

- Application input into the bank's system by on-site employee.
- Instant pre-approval evaluation done. If documents are present, instant approval is possible.
- Bank employee handles all paper work and, if request is for a sales finance POS loan, gives applicant a loan verification document which can be used at the cashier's desk as partial or full payment for the goods to be purchased.
- If request is for a non-POS loan, funds are disbursed as per following section.

Funds disbursement options

- Into applicant's bank account (at any bank).
- By cheque to be cashed at Post Office or other banks.
- Amount placed on a non-embossed card that can be used at any ATM to draw the funds down. Would likely need to offer first 2–3 withdrawals free in case other banks levy a charge for 'off us' withdrawals.

Loan repayment options

- By funds transfer from customer's account at any bank, to our bank. By standing order or pre-authorised debit.
- At Post Offices in cash, as one would pay standard utility invoices.
- In cash at special 'bill payment' cashiers or centres if available in the country. Note that there may be a charge for this service which the customer has to pay.

Figure 4.1 illustrates how to design an appropriate process map. To keep things simple, we assumed no broker channels, only included one product and only covered the upfront part of the process (origination, approval, start of disbursement).

Figure 4.1: Personal loan sales and operations process design – retail store and direct sourced

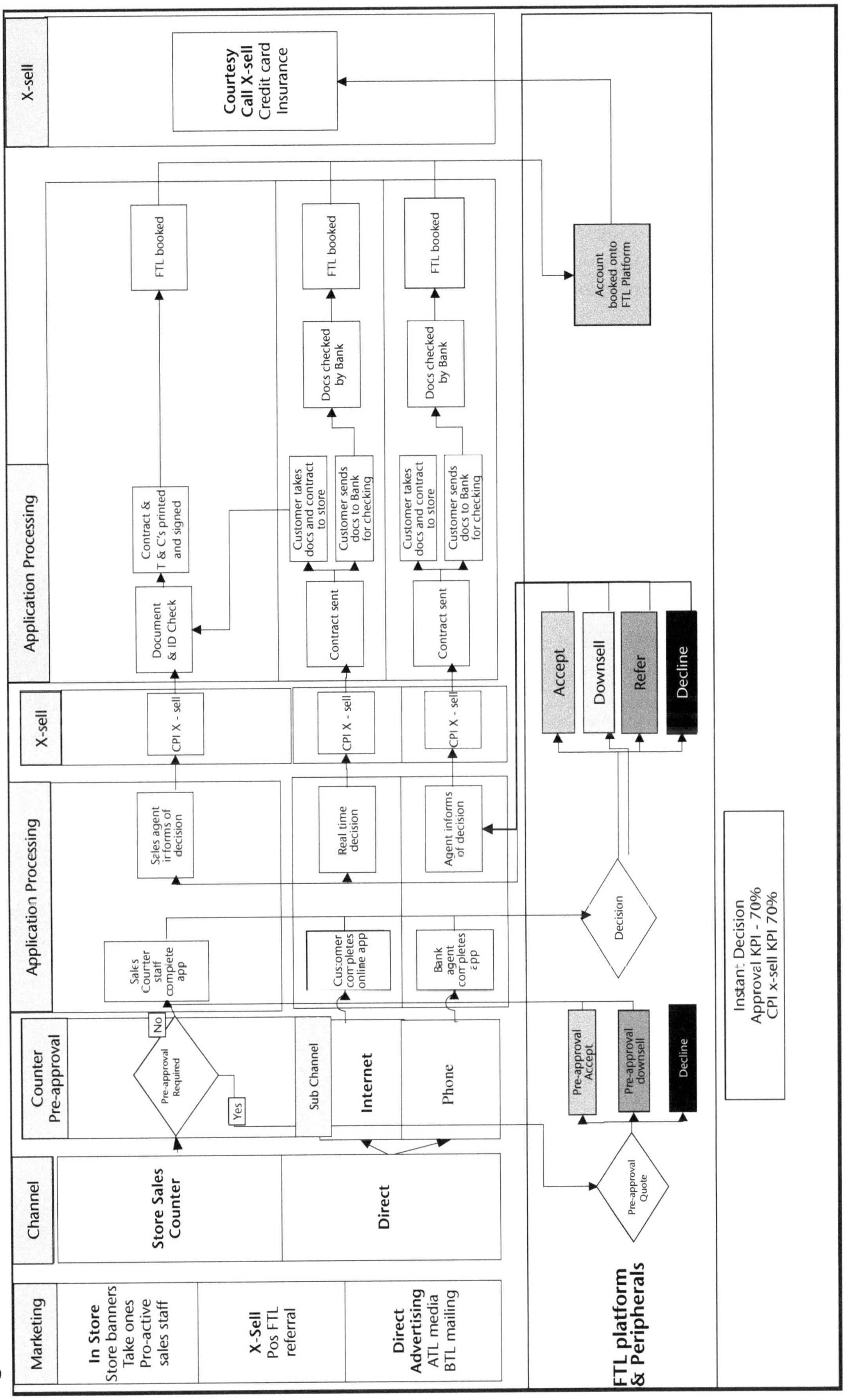

Source: 3-i Inc.

There are two other, crucial, elements to intermediary relationships that need to be integrated into our process designs. They are related to customer ownership and communication with customers.

Customer ownership

This is a key issue and has to be allowed for in processes, contracts, operational and IT set-ups.

Who owns the customer and to what extent? As a general rule, if a customer is brought in via an intermediary, the intermediary should be allowed to cross-sell to that customer any other product he is allowed to sell. The bank should not attempt to proactively cross-sell products offered by the intermediary, but should be able to respond to a request by the customer. Who ends up with the customer as his own if the partnership breaks down is just as important.

Communicating through intermediaries

Good intermediaries will want to be able to service effectively the customers they bring in. This means they need to know where customer applications are at any moment. They will also want to be able to communicate updates and results regarding accounts opened, loans granted, etc. to the customers first. This requires flexibility on the bank's part, trust, and IT/operations set-ups to accommodate.

At its simplest level, application processing needs to include a tracking system that can provide status information to allowed third parties. Processes also must be in place to proactively feed key information to the intermediaries first if that is what has been agreed. That is, our usual customer communication process needs to incorporate and integrate communication via third parties, within the confines of regulations and our own policies.

Partner selection

General alliance building guidelines were reviewed at the beginning of this chapter. We will focus here on some specific issues related to intermediaries and, especially, sales finance partnerships with retailers.

As the first rule, one must have a templated approach to screening potential intermediaries and an agreed business plan design to evaluate the opportunities. A simplified preliminary assessment checklist for a potential retail alliance partner is shown in Table 4.1.

Table 4.1: POS sales finance partner selection and approach checklist

1. **Our ability to serve their needs?**
    a. Have we got the products their customers need?
    b. Can we also offer solutions to their employees?
2. **Existing business potential?**
    a. Size of their customer base and its fit to our offer? (e.g. need for loans, ability to repay, good demographics).
    b. Current and projected sales? Percentage of sales needing sales finance offer?
3. **Brand strength?**
    a. Are they well known and reputable?
    b. Are they likely to remain so?
4. **New opportunity?**
    a. If 2 and 3 above do not apply, is it a promising new start-up with good potential that existing major retailers ignored?
    b. What proof do we have for this (e.g. market research)?
5. **Competitive opportunity?**
    a. No existing financial partner?
    b. Potential to replace existing one (e.g. relationship issues, contract for renewal, better offer from us)?
6. **Ability to negotiate at HQ level?**
    a. Can we sign deal at the centre?
    b. To what extent do we need to sell co-operation to individual stores?

Source: 3-i Inc.

A more detailed, more numerical template would also cover the information shown in Table 4.2.

Table 4.2: Additional POS sales finance partner selection checklist

1. Name of company.
2. Location – country, region.
3. Owner – name, country, percentage share.
4. Outlets and their sizes in target market.
5. Type of business.
6. Current sales finance partner and end of contract.
7. Status with current partner.
8. Any relationship with our bank – corporate, consumer, etc.
9. Their product needs.
10. Our product offer.
11. Yearly turnover and percentage we could get.
12. Estimated yearly volumes for our offers for first three years.
13. Our upfront cost/effort needed.
14. Commission and support needs.
15. Status of negotiations.
16. Next steps.
17. Other information – e.g. worldwide outlets, opportunities in other areas, legal issues, etc.

Source: 3-i Inc.

It also useful to have our own benchmarks, or hurdle rates, established upfront to avoid spending time on potential opportunities that will not qualify in the end. Understandably, hurdles rates may differ for different types of intermediaries. For relationships that require individual targeting and customisation effort we need to have higher benchmarks than for yet another white goods retailer which we can serve with existing offers and processes. The examples in Table 4.3 are from a mid-sized Western European bank, in a mid-sized market, offering personal loans.

Table 4.3: Sales expectations

Minimum annual sales expectations by the bank, by year 3 (€)	
New alliance partner, from the 'other' category	15m
New major retail partner (national chain)	8m
New small retail partner (large single store or regional chain)	5m
New broker or other financial intermediary	3m

Source: 3-i Inc.

IT requirements

Building on what we reviewed in Chapter 2, the following checklist provides a high-level systems requirements overview to allow a bank to handle third-party, intermediary-driven sales and service:

1. Ability to allow graduated access to the system, in terms of information access, allowed activities, differentiated by customer, individual sales staff, intermediary offices and staff.
2. Sales and commission tracking, allowing individual-level tracking of sales and referrals across multiple channels. Also, ability to split commission among different intermediaries and at multi-level: sales agent, office, headquarters (of intermediaries).
3. Ability to integrate intermediaries' processes and systems into the bank's operating and CRM set-ups, without major changes on either side.
4. Application and customer tracking to allow updates on where sales leads or account openings are at any given point, based on multiple variables (e.g. their source).
5. Customer contact tracking to allow differentiating between reactive and proactive sales at individual staff member level.
6. Flexible communication process with all its enablers, allowing customer communication both directly and via intermediary staff.
7. Strong fraud protection and audit trail set-ups.

It is hoped, as with all the other chapters, that the preceding summary of setting up and managing sales through third-party intermediaries will help the practitioner in a very hands-on way. Due to the limitations of just one chapter on the topic all aspects may not have been covered. Anyone wishing for more information should feel free to contact me.

Chapter 5

Remote electronic channels: the limits of cost efficiency

Searching finance

Traditional electronic channels

Overview

Sales and service channels come in many varieties: branches, branch agents, sales agents, kiosks, call centres, third-party or alliance sales forces, internet banking, website access, mobile phone banking, ATMs, direct mail, consumer finance (indirect loans) and many more. In many cases discussions are still taking place whether something should be considered a channel or a business or a marketing tool.

Think of consumer finance: if it is a channel, then acquiring customers who make no money for the bank is acceptable because it means new acquisitions cost zero – very good efficiency. If it is a business unit, then of course acquiring customers who make no money for the bank is not acceptable at all. (My perspective is that on a standalone basis, for a consumer finance company, it should be a business. For a full service bank it should be treated as an acquisition channel.)

Or consider direct mail. Is it simply a marketing tool, or is it a channel because one can acquire customers through it directly, without involving other channels? Wherever the discussions lead, contact channels (those parts of the bank through which prospects and customers can contact the bank or can be contacted, whether for sales or service needs) need to be integrated with each other in a customer-centric way, but also in a way that is profitable to the bank. Every channel, every product, every segment must be profitable on its own, on an ongoing basis, for any retail bank to survive long term.

Another area of discussion is where to draw the line between different channel types. Traditional channels used to mean branches only, but telephone banking is so embedded now in most banks that it may be hard to argue that it is still an alternative channel. Similarly, if one defines traditional channels as those with physical presence and face-to-face personal contact with customers, then some new developments such as branch agents and sales agents classify as traditional, despite their novelty. It might be better to differentiate between remote, direct and physical channels, where for example branches would be 'physical', sales agents 'direct' and phone banking 'remote'.

This approach also supports the philosophy of 'acquire direct, service remotely, build relationships in person (i.e. face-to-face in an actual physical setting)'. Whichever way a bank defines its channel set-up, it is hard to argue that internet, mobile banking and phone banking are basically both remote and alternative channels. Given the ongoing dominance of physical outlet-based banking in most areas, these newer channels need to be integrated into the overall structure and should not be expected to fully replace a physical presence soon.

Main types, roles and evolution

Channels may have different roles. For new channels these roles would normally evolve in a logical, layered way. That is, some features come before others. The following list reviews the key roles channels can have, in the sequence in which they would normally evolve. That is, when a new channel is established it will usually follow the process of offering #1, then #2, then #3 and so on. This is done in a way that new functionalities are added to the already existing ones – layered on:

1. Passive information – information is made available in a 'canned' version and is available on request.
2. Interactive information – information can be requested in an interactive way, 'what if' questions are answered.
3. Sales facilitation – account opening forms or actual account opening can be requested, follow-up can be asked for, appointment booking through other channels is possible.
4. Services – transactions can be initiated, customer or account information change is possible.
5. Reactive sales – a banking relationship can actually be started at the prospect's request, or a new product sold at the customer's request.
6. Proactive sales – the bank can undertake proactive selling through this channel, ideally being able also to conclude the sales (open the account or relationship).

This evolution process gives guidance on adding features to existing channels and setting the development direction for evolving channels.

Telephone banking

Phone banking (call centre) is a straightforward example. If one wants to gradually build capabilities in such a set-up, one would likely build it as follows:

- In-bound calls only, information is provided. This will allow basic services and awareness building;
- In-bound calls only, with sales facilitation. This level, for example, is required if the bank sells products where use may need to be stopped (e.g. credit cards) – the call centre must be able to take the information, verify it and follow up on it;
- Services – for transactional services an interactive voice response (IVR) system is likely needed to manage call volumes;
- In-bound, reactive sales – accounts can be opened through the telephone banking centre;
- Out-bound, proactive sales – active prospecting and follow-up on sales activities initiated by other areas such as Marketing or Sales.

Internet banking

Internet banking also developed along the lines shown above, from simple website access and information availability to fully fledged banking services and sales offers triggered by customer profile and activity analysis ('interactive one-on-one marketing'). Internet banking, in my opinion, shows how spectacularly wrong the whole global banking industry can get things, by forgetting about its reason for being: the consumer.

Banks first tried to position internet offers on 'savings'. However, because (credit loss adjusted) bank margins usually move between 1 and 3%, the savings offered could only be very small. A '0.25% lower rate' sounds pretty meagre in an environment of '25% off!' advertising in supermarkets.

Next came 'bells and whistles' – chat rooms, community sites, related (and unrelated) offers. Of course, in the spirit of trying to force migration to this new, low-cost channel, cross-references to other channels were ignored. Many sites did not even give phone numbers to call in case of questions, presenting a 'mail back' option instead. For those of us who have forgotten: company internet connections tended to block e-mails to websites in the beginning. And most people used internet access at work to log into their bank sites...

Finally, after two failed attempts, we have listened to consumers. We have heard what they want: convenience (24/7, anywhere access), information (on rates, payments, branch locations, hours, etc) and basic services. We provided these. And the internet banking boom has started...

ATMs

ATM banking shows a similar layering trend as internet banking. But it started with transactions ('services'), added 'information' (about account balances and activities first), then added extra banking services (e.g. funds transfers, investments, loans requests, electronic purse refills), then services from other providers (such as mobile phone card refills), finally adding on-screen advertising and proactive sales.

Kiosks

Kiosks have been around for a long time, with the first financial services kiosk introduced about 25 years ago in the US by First National Bank of Chicago. They have had a mixed reception. Several banks, especially in North America, have closed kiosks in the recent past – Bank of Montreal (BMO) and CIBC/Amicus of Canada have both closed their supermarket kiosk networks in Canada and the US, and First American Credit union lasted all of nine months with its kiosk experiment before shutting it down. On the other hand, both ING and Alpha Bank (of Greece) have not so long ago started kiosks up (in for example Romania and Poland) with good reported success. Why the difference?

Different levels of success can be traced to three areas:

- Environment – branch saturation;
- Positioning – sales versus service;
- Definition – 'high-end ATM' versus true two-way remote banking.

Both BMO and CIBC have extended branch coverage in Canada, and kiosks could not add much to this. On the other hand, Alpha Bank and ING have been building their presence in Central and Eastern Europe, so kiosks are a natural, low-cost addition.

Another difference is that both BMO and CIBC focused on supermarket presence, where most of the activities were service oriented, such as cash withdrawals and inquiries. Offering foreign exchange (for a fee), credit applications or insurance options helped ING and Alpha.

Finally, many banks still define kiosks as high-end ATMs, instead of a truly interactive environment as they should be. The latter would have, for example, live video feed from a remote location, instant direct banking access and more. Sales opportunities with a 'true kiosk' are many times greater than with a simple high-end ATM.

Challenges

Channel integration is one challenge and may not be the greatest. Well-designed plans and processes will integrate channels by default, as long as the organisational set-up allows this. In addition, having a robust CRM platform will also serve to tie channels together, by making all customer information available at all contact points and sorting out follow-up on leads and customer care among the different channels.

The balance of sales and service and shifting from one to the other may be a bigger challenge for all channels, not only newer ones. How the overall role is defined for a call centre (is it a service centre, a phone bank, a business development function, all of these?) and how the roles within such a call centre are defined can generate a lot of debate. Should a sales kiosk offer cash in / out at the counter because customers require it ('service') or should it focus on new sales only? (Author's recommendation: no personal cash handling for cost / security reasons. ATMs with cash in / out capability can solve this dilemma.)

The strategic positioning of new channels and expectations from them are another challenge for the banking industry. Again, a somewhat disappointing case study in this area is the evolution of internet banking:

- As all would now probably agree, internet banking is primarily a relationship building tool, not a tool for new acquisitions. While 'shoppers' may log on to get information, the ability of banks to convince prospects to open accounts through the internet remains low;
- It is convenience driven, not price driven. It allows access at any time, to any account information. On the other hand, the margins in retail banking do not allow the kind of '50% off' offers that drive the business of price-focused retailers;
- Information content and ease of use are the key requirements, not add-ons which can be better obtained elsewhere (travel bookings, e-mail, chat rooms – real examples).

Addressing the challenges

Channel integration challenges, while often talked about, are not being addressed as discussed earlier.

The balance of sales and service requires careful role definitions, capacity planning and a customer-centric approach. Take call centres / phone banking as an example.

Role definitions point in the direction of both sales and service, so it should satisfy both. Capacity planning and a customer-centric approach would go hand-in-hand, as follows:

- Respect for customer needs, and sales efficiencies, would suggest one central number to call, not many. It is simply easier to remember. If possible, it should be a toll-free number. If calls outside of the toll-free area are expected, an alternate number must also be provided. Many local toll-free numbers cannot be accessed from abroad.
- Calls should be 'streamed off' early, separating out VIP customers, small and medium-sized enterprises (SMEs), other customers and prospects. This allows for quicker access and better service for all. Entry into the system should not be restricted by requiring personal identification that may not be quickly, or at all, available. Note that some international phone banking centres still require local ID numbers from their international target segments – which they clearly do not have – to allow access. One can imagine the frustration on the consumer's part and the lost sales opportunity on the bank's.
- If the call is answered by an IVR system, the number of options should not be more than four. Most people do not remember more options and only get confused. Quickly cutting to a personal representative should also be an option both upfront and at any stage of the IVR engagement.
- Outbound calling should be handled by a different team. However, for capacity planning flexibility, team members should be able to handle incoming calls when needed.
- Please also see the service quality standards as outlined in Appendix C, at the end of Chapter 6, for more pointers.

The issues around strategic positioning can be best reviewed using internet banking as an example. A number of key answers have already been provided above under 'Challenges'. Internet banking should be convenience driven, relationship focused, and providing information and services that consumers want. Having said that, a couple of other items are worth mentioning.

First, the basics need to be covered. Language options should be provided if needed and default settings should be easy to override to allow consumer choice. Contact information needs to be prominently provided (e.g. call centre phone number) in case a personal contact is needed. Pages should be easy and fast to load and print. Care should be taken, allowing for blocks existing in many corporate servers. A fact of life is that many customers access their internet banking site from work. Some servers block mail back options, others block images, etc. Everyday language needs to be used – let us call internet banking 'internet banking'; any other fancy marketing name may just be confusing. And, of course, navigation must be dead easy.

Second, the real potential of the internet may still be waiting to be exploited. For example, the technology exists to set up and track individual investment portfolios via internet banking sites. Technology also allows for flags, automatic messages to be generated or standing orders to be activated based on different variables. Market indices can also be tracked. All in all, every tool is available to build a 'private bank' for the mass affluent segment via the internet.

Building individual 'mutual funds', triggering market-driven investment changes and getting updates on portfolio and market activities can all be delivered at a low cost for large groups of people. Most of these services have so far only been available to the very wealthy, through private banking offers. This may well be the next wave of the internet banking revolution – if the industry does it right this time.

New types of electronic channels

There are a number of new channel developments in the electronic domain. Let us review a few obvious, and not so obvious ones, grouping these initiatives into:

- Mobile (phone) banking;
- New internet developments;
- Social media-based channels.

The key thing to remember is: real world rules apply. That is, just because we are moving in a 'virtual world', we are still real people, acting as we would always do. New electronic channels and the so-called 'new media' are only tools, not a new reality. It is still real people who are using them, with their needs, emotions and rationales. Forget this at your peril – as many failed companies have done.

Mobile banking

Mobile banking, or rather 'mobile-phone banking', is finding its niche these days. Mobile phones are used for:

- Paying bills (for parking, for charitable donations, for music downloads and more);
- Security confirmations (to confirm credit card transactions or to provide added password protection for electronic funds transfers via SMS);
- Sending urgent, short reminders (about maturing investments, important market changes).

An interesting development is that mobile phone banking seems to be advancing fastest in Europe and the Asia / Africa developing world, as opposed to North America. High mobile penetrations and the predominance of electronic fund transfers in Europe (as opposed to cheques in North America) are one reason for this. Lack of land-based phone infrastructure in the developing world is another.

We'll have to see what the future brings with the many possibilities linked to 3G and 4G smart phones. However, in the words of one insurance executive, "nobody wants to read his insurance policy on a phone screen". But there still remain many possible applications to be introduced. Who wouldn't want to know when a credit card payment or loan payment is due? When a term deposit is coming up for maturity? When a sudden market change creates an investment opportunity? How many banks are doing these today?

New internet developments

These include:

- Virtual money;
- Virtual banking;
- Peer-to-peer (P2P) banking.

At the same time, a much-hyped development of the past few years – financial aggregation – seems to have gone nowhere. Security concerns and the fear of losing control prevented it from gaining wide acceptance. 'Real world rules' have won over technologically driven convenience offers.

Virtual money

Virtual money means 'PayPal' to most (see below for 'Linden Dollars'). PayPal, owned by eBay, provides an electronic payment ability over the internet from a virtual internet account. This account can be filled up from, and emptied into, real world payment tools such as credit card or bank accounts, or be accessed via paper cheques in North America.

The benefit of PayPal is essentially added security. By separating a limited amount of funds into a standalone account, and by using the added security features of that account, people paying through PayPal put an additional block between their 'real world' accounts and potential intruders.

Virtual banking

Virtual banking has been championed by Second Life. Banks in the Second Life cyberspace used another type of virtual money, 'Linden $', which could be converted to/from real dollars. This virtual banking scene was devastated even faster and sooner than the real world's, in the latest 'Great Recession'.

Ginko Financial, a speculative Second Life bank collapsed in 2007 and brought many more down with it. Linden Lab, owner / creator of Second Life then had to ban banking and ATMs in its virtual domain to avoid a PR and liability disaster. Only banks that are regulated in the real world are today allowed to operate in Second Life. This turn of events is rather unfortunate because there are many possible banking innovations that could be offered through virtual banks.

Peer-to-peer banking

P2P banking is one new development enabled by internet technology. It has been with us in an electronic version since 2005, when zopa.com and kiva.org started. A quick look at these two leading sites gives a good overview of P2P's capabilities.

Zopa matches people with excess money to those with borrowing needs, cutting out the usual intermediary – the bank. Lenders get a higher return and borrowers a lower rate, by splitting the profit the bank would normally clear for managing the funds transfer. However, it is worth remembering that the bank also takes on the credit risk for the money it charges for arranging a deposit-to-loan deal. While getting more for their money, lenders in P2P give up the guarantee banks would provide on their deposits (by taking over the credit risk).

Kiva is an interesting segment of P2P. It combines microfinance (such as Grameen Bank) with P2P (like Zopa). Investors / donors can pool their funds via a web-enabled platform, which then be allocated (with a say from the investors) to entrepreneurs in developing economies.

Social media-based channels

These include Facebook, LinkedIn, MySpace and other 'social aggregator' sites. While one can use them as selling or prospecting channels, a few rules need to be kept in mind:

1. Social media is 'body intensive' as opposed to 'money intensive' for a bank to enter. Social media requires ongoing instant involvement that only live people can provide. It is not enough to allocate a sales or marketing budget or buy the latest technology, one needs to allocate FTE – full-time equivalent (people). Given the fact that it is much more difficult to get a headcount increase approved than an extra budget request, setting up a properly functioning 'social media channel group' will likely be an uphill battle for any sales manager.
2. Make sure your target segment is 'involved' with the media. Senior managers may use LinkedIn but have no time for Twitter. CEOs may be on Facebook to keep in touch with family and friends around the world but screen out all but essential e-mail and other messages.
3. Real world rules apply. Only real people have the need for banking services. And while they use virtual tools they remain real, with real needs and emotions. This point is amply illustrated by a recent Nielsen survey, in which people were asked what types of messages they trust (see Figure 5.1). Personal ones, whether face-to-face or on the web, had the highest trust level. Traditional media channels came next. The only new media message type that came near (matching the bottom end of traditional media) was e-mails people actually signed up for receiving. Even ads for related products, generated by search engines, came much lower in terms of trust than good old TV...

Figure 5.1:People completely or somewhat trusting forms of advertising (%)

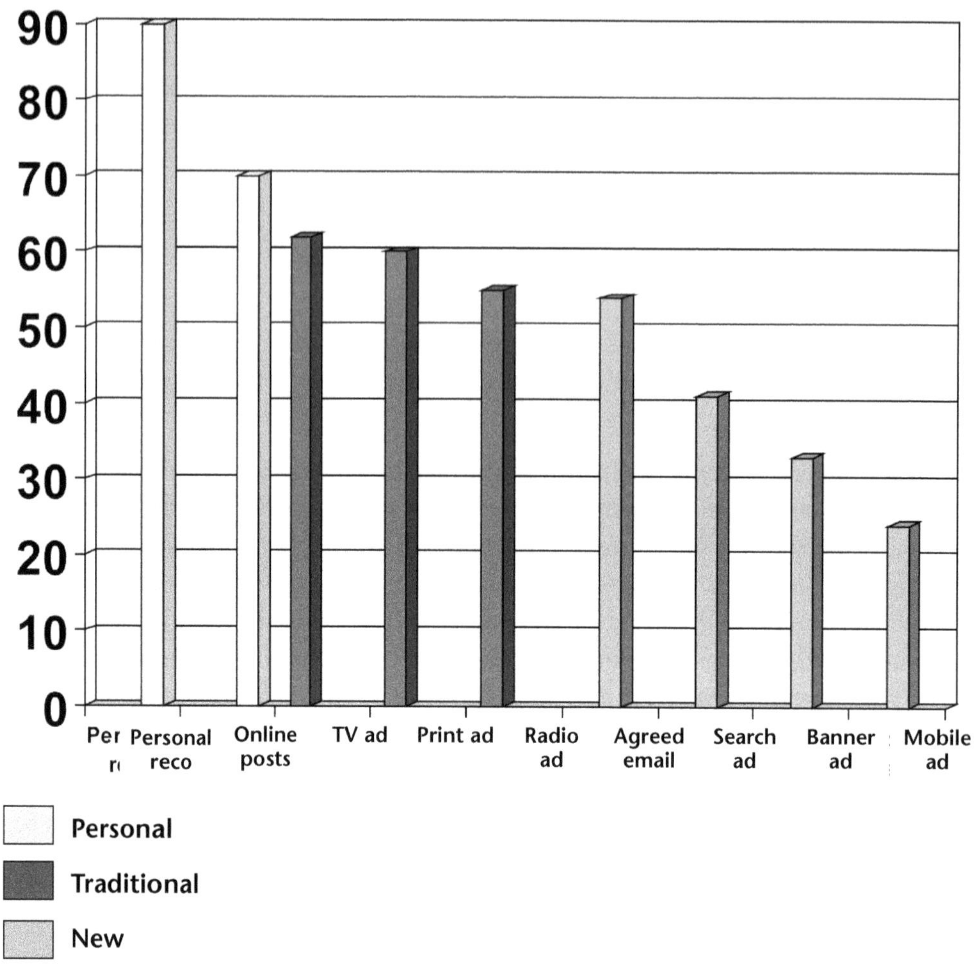

(Source: The Nielsen Company / Randall Beard)

Chapter 6

Buying, managing and controlling your channels

Searching finance

Introduction

So far we have talked mostly about building, integrating and managing different distribution channel types. But our review of channels would not be complete without touching on three additional areas: mergers and acquisitions (M&A), customer relationship management (CRM) and service quality (SQ).

First, what if we were to buy distribution? What role should sales management play in evaluating M&A opportunities? Second, CRM is, in essence, the ultimate channel integration initiative. What should Sales expect from it? Finally, how do we set the right expectations in terms of customer service quality across the different channels?

Mergers and acquisitions – buying your channels

From a sales efficiency perspective, existing M&A models are inadequate. They would normally take into account the value of a product portfolio and a few additional factors, usually related to credit risks, strategic fit, market development, value of tangible and intangible assets. However, the value of the acquisition target's customer base, *without* (and independent of) their holdings with the bank, is mostly ignored. The same goes for most other channel (acquisition type) related items.

Because it takes more time, effort and expense to sell the same offer to a cold prospect than to an existing customer, the value of existing relationships (independent of holdings) needs to be estimated. Only this can ensure a true valuation of M&A targets. This perspective is very much a sales / marketing-driven view and therefore it falls to the Sales and Marketing departments to proactively influence M&A discussions, using this philosophy.

With the same approach in mind, one can expand the Sales and Marketing M&A evaluation to other areas. For example, the value of intermediary contacts, the prospects database of the bank to be acquired, its sales personnel and its third-party sales contracts in force can all add or subtract from its value. This section will review some of the key components when evaluating an acquisition target with sales efficiency and channel differences in mind. A few additional areas will also be mentioned, but not detailed, for the sake of completeness. A short guide on assigning values to customer and prospect bases and the like is included in Appendix A at the chapter end for quick reference.

Due diligence checklist

Key areas for investigation should include:

- Overall business strategy;
- Sales and marketing;
- Channels (sales and service);
- Credit products;

- Liability (deposit) products;
- Personnel;
- IT and other.

Overall business strategy fit

1. Mission — Vision — Strategy;
2. Target customer description/profile;
3. Size of target market;
4. Sales and marketing strategy;
5. Sales activity (branch based, alternative sourcing);
6. Product portfolio.

Marketing and sales review

Customer base

We need to understand size, type (quality) and profitability. The value of the base *without* product holdings needs to be estimated. This value should reflect the benefit of having the customer in our system and having had previous relationship with him, which should make future cross-selling easier. The value should *not* reflect what we make on his holdings with us today. Information to be gathered should include:

- Number of customers;
- Number of accounts;
- Demographics (age, gender, income, occupation, education, family status and size);
- Cost per customer (acquisition costs);
- Product holdings, cross-sell rates;
- Direct or indirect customer;
- Vintage (how long a customer, repurchased product or not);
- Lifestyle data (car and home ownership, travel, etc);
- Channel usage (branch, external sales, phone, internet, etc);
- Perception (satisfaction with service level);
- Contact details (address, phone number) if available;
- Psychographics if available (attitude information);
- Any research info available from customer research;
- Attrition number and rate;
- Account dormancy trends;

- Credit data, e.g. credit scores, credit history, etc.

Value to be assigned to the existing customer base:

- 65% of the acquisition cost (AC) of the same customer by the bank. This is normally the difference between the cost of cross-selling to an existing customer and acquiring the same customer, with the same product offer.

Prospect base

This involves the same approach as for the customer base and needs the same information. The bank also needs to know how the prospect list was generated, whether it comprises for example former customers, a purchased list, indirect customers, or an affiliate's base. In addition, the bank needs to know whether there are any limitations on the use of the base (e.g. time limit, privacy protection limit, 'ownership of names' issues).

Value can be assigned to prospects either by estimating how much it would cost to buy the same quality list in the market, or by assigning a percentage of average AC:

- Former direct customers – 50% of AC (acquisition cost of same customer by the bank);
- Former indirect customers – 15% of AC;
- Affiliate's customers – 15–25% of AC (higher value if affiliate is branded the same);
- Other – 5–15% of AC (higher value if already contacted and responded positively).

Intermediary contacts

These can be many different types:

- Retailers (e.g. granting indirect loans);
- Estate agents (e.g. providing mortgage referrals);
- Thought leaders (e.g. accountancy firms referring investment prospects);
- External sales agents (e.g. financial advisers selling insurance), etc.

Their value will depend on how good the relationship is and how much it would cost to develop the same relationship with the given intermediary.

Value can be estimated in the range of 3–10 times average customer acquisition cost, for example:

- Retailer set-up for granting loans – 5 x AC;
- Estate agent contact – 3 x AC;
- Lawyer with history of investment referrals – 10 x AC.

External sales force value estimation is better done by reviewing their contract status and assigning value (if any) based on that.

Brand strength

1. Information to be gathered includes:
   - Unaided awareness;
   - Aided awareness;
   - Brand image (from research);
   - Historical information (i.e. changes in image and awareness).
2. Unaided awareness drives branch traffic, aided awareness drives direct acquisition effectiveness, image drives overall marketing and sales effectiveness.
3. Check for consistency between our image and the M&A candidate's image.
4. Unaided awareness is the toughest measure. It is enough to estimate the brand's value using this measure if the images are not too different.
5. Use media costs and both internal and competitive info in the market to estimate what it would cost us to build the same awareness.
6. For guidance, unaided awareness below 5% has very limited value. 10–15% represents value. It would normally cost €5–10m in total media spending over three years, in a developed market of 10m, to reach 15% unaided awareness.

Caution:

- Awareness should be measured among target customers, not overall;
- If images are different, the brand's value needs to be reduced or eliminated. If the image is positive but different, reduce the brand value assigned by 50%. If the image is negative (from our perspective), reduce the brand value to zero.

Marketing infrastructure

1. Key components:
   - Marketing database;
   - CRM set up;
   - Software packages in use.
2. Key information needs to be gathered on:
   - Customer relationship view – yes/no;
   - Customer and prospect contact details and contact history – yes/no;
   - Customer and prospect history, how long, what elements tracked;
   - Prospect base handling capability in database – yes/no;
   - Customer value indicator – yes/no;
   - Credit information and history, what type of information;
   - Marketing / sales / phone centre / other channels linked – yes/no;
   - Analytical capability, what kind of package.

Distribution and service channels

Service and delivery channels used:

- Procedures and processes:
    - Operational procedures and workflows;
    - Checks and controls (e.g. money laundering, fraud prevention, etc);
    - Complaints log;
    - Customer claims;
    - Efficiency records (including service levels);
    - Outsourced services and agreements with third-party suppliers;
- Outlets/branches:
    - Number of physical outlets (branches);
    - Quality of premises (location and appearance);
    - Number of own and leased premises (terms and conditions);
    - Average size of outlet (customers, staff and assets/liabilities);
    - Average cost for rebuilding/redecoration/refurbishment;
- ATMs:
    - Number of ATMs installed (on premise/off premise);
    - Which make (vendor) and models;
    - ATM management in-house or outsourced (if in-house, using what software package; if outsourced, to whom and under what contractual terms and conditions);
    - Number of ATM transactions per month/year (by type);
    - Average cost per machine;
- Call centre:
    - Technology used (vendor, IVR, etc.);
    - Number of workstations installed;
    - Number of agents employed;
    - Service offered to customers (24/7);
    - Number of calls handled (monthly, annually);
    - Type of calls (by numbers);
    - Average duration of a call;
    - Size of investment for set-up;
- Electronic banking:
    - Technology used for internet banking;

- Service offered online (balance inquiry, transaction inquiry, statement, money transfers, standing orders, etc);
- Number of customers online;
- Number of online transactions by type;
- Number of online support staff (customer service and technical);
- Size of investment for online set-up;
- Technology used for mobile banking;
- Services offered via mobile phone (SMS, alerts, balance inquiry, transactions, etc);
- Number of customers using mobile banking;
- Number of mobile banking transactions by type;
- Number of support staff for mobile banking (customer service and technical);
- Size of investment for mobile banking set-up;

◆ Other emerging channels:

- Which channels, gather information;
- New channels to be implemented within next 6–12 months.

Consider also the integration of different channels, i.e. are they all connected, with full customer view and same operational capabilities or not?

Value should be assigned based on how much it would cost us to build the same set-up.

There is a need to take into account real estate lease clauses, location quality and similar criteria for branches.

Consider also the connectedness of different channels, i.e. are they all connected, with full customer view and same operational capabilities or not?

Credit risk management / lending products portfolio

1. Risk policies:
   - Approach, development and implementation;
   - List of policies by product (including valuation of collateral);
   - List of policies by process (e.g. application process leading to identification, authentication; decision-making process, collections, etc);
2. Risk management process:
   - Authority of head office versus branches for credit decisions;
   - Responsibility for monitoring of loan portfolio;
   - Responsibility for collections;

3. Loan portfolio:
    - Breakdown of the portfolio by:
        - Primary source of applicants;
        - Socio-demographics of applicants;
        - Type and number of loans;
        - Type and amounts of loans;
        - Average size by type of loan;
        - Original term (tenor) by type and volume;
        - Average tenor by type and volume;
        - Fixed versus variable interest rate by type and volume;
        - Local versus foreign currency loans (currency clauses);
        - Number and volume of loans rolled over (used to repay due loans);
    - Delinquencies by (always number and volume):
        - Age of loan (months on book);
        - Days delinquent (categories: in order, five days in arrears, up to 30 days in arrears, thereafter in 30-day increments);
        - Reason of delinquency (illness, unemployment, exchange rate, etc);
    - Development of delinquencies (specifically flow rates) according to the same criteria as above;
    - Number and volume of delinquent loans in repayment programmes;
    - Type and volume of collateral (evaluation process);
4. Collections:
    - Number and volume of loans in 'soft/early collections';
    - Number and volume of loans in 'hard collections';
    - Collection efficiency in terms of recovery (amounts and time);
    - Number of court cases pending (by type of loan);
5. Loan loss provisions:
    - Provisioning and write-off policies;
    - Specific provisions created for above delinquency ranges;
    - General provisions created;
    - Number and amounts of loans written off (by year).

Savings and deposits products portfolio

Breakdown of the deposit portfolio by:

- Type:

  - Current accounts (corporate/retail by number and volume);
  - Savings accounts;
  - Deposit accounts;
  - Other accounts;
- Corporate deposits:
  - Number and volume;
  - Average deposit size;
  - Breakdown by currency;
  - Term/maturity analysis;
  - Breakdown by amounts (ranges);
  - 20 largest deposits;
- Retail savings accounts:
  - Number and volume;
  - Average deposit size;
  - Breakdown by currency;
  - Term/maturity analysis;
  - Breakdown by amounts (ranges);
  - 20 largest savings;
- Retail deposits:
  - Number and volume;
  - Average deposit size;
  - Breakdown by currency;
  - Term/maturity analysis;
  - Breakdown by amounts (ranges);
  - 20 largest savings.

Personnel

1. Organisational structure (including job descriptions);
2. Staff numbers;
3. Management / staff ratios;
4. Age, education and experience;
5. Compensation structure;
6. Recruitment and retention policy (including staff fluctuation);
7. Absence and disciplinary records;

8. Training, policy and implementation;
9. Performance management and appraisal system (recognition and reward).

Value assigned can be estimated at six times monthly earnings for staff considered. This is composed of 3x salary as recruitment cost; 1x salary as training costs; 1x salary as management time saved; 1x salary as efficiency loss avoided by keeping the same (good) staff for continuity in customer relations, etc.

Information technology, other

The IT area is not in the scope of this publication. It needs a separate approach and review.

Customer relationship management – managing your channels

Definition

CRM is the ultimate channel integration, done from a customer perspective. It deserves a separate section because there is still a lot of confusion about what CRM is and is not. It is useful to start with a concise definition:

- CRM optimises the acquisition, relationship building and retention processes to maximise profit per customer;
- It creates an optimal full cycle of managing the bank's interaction with its future and present customers, through all channels / contact points;
- It links all processes and operationalises them for high-quality, no-exception execution;
- It makes the job of sales people easier.

On the other hand, CRM is not:

- A sales force automation (SFA) or call centre management system;
- A technology platform, software, hardware, etc;
- Automating existing processes (without optimising them first).

Key issues

following are some frequent issues with CRM implementation which can pretty much ensure sales efficiency gains will not be utilised:

1. Defining and treating CRM as any of the three definitions above of what CRM is not;
2. Ignoring the alignments needed for proper implementation:
   - Strategic;
   - Organisational;
   - Process;

3. Using the CRM system as a front-end link to operations, instead of as a 'wrapper' around operational links;
4. Ignoring time required for selling the idea and time required for training once the system is up and running;
5. Implementing it in such a way that it will make the sales staff's life more difficult. For example:
    - No single log-in within a security shell;
    - No navigation rules requiring 'any new piece of information to be three clicks away or less';
    - Not allowing experienced sales staff to ignore prescribed sales process and scripting when they know better;
    - Requiring multiple data entry, instead of automatic updates of all information fields with data already entered;
6. Over engineering – trying to do everything at once, covering all options upfront, instead of planning for a gradual introduction and scaling up in capacity and features as business requires.

Benefits

Done right, CRM should create significant benefits, about two-thirds of which can be calculated in advance, applying the so-called 'process mapping' approach to current business practices:

- Reviewing all key processes that lead to customer acquisition, relationship building and retention;
- Identifying where inefficiencies and breaks occur – most often these happen when the process crosses departmental lines,
- Defining what needs to be changed, how the CRM set-up would facilitate this, what the costs of this would be and what the improvements would generate in terms of extra business or efficiencies.

The remaining third of benefits would include future efficiency gains, which are hard to define based on existing processes. They could include, for example, the following sales-related benefits:

- Being able to link internal and external variables to drive actions. For example, correlating stock market moves with customers' investment activities. By predicting which segment will react which way, targeted sales activities can offer them different products depending on market sentiment (e.g. offer a deposit alternative to those who sell their mutual funds when markets go down; offer other funds to those who buy into the market when it declines, offer investment advice to those who hold tight during downturns).
- Mixing sales / marketing processes with operational / credit processes. For example, being able to track pending credit applications (pre-approvals) and doing automated follow-ups before prospects lose interest.

- Reducing errors, saving on reworks. By reducing human input (data transfer) and by operationalising processes, the chance of human error is reduced and rework in Sales, Operations, etc, are cut.
- Cutting sales session times. Cutting sales times and increasing capacity by having a relationship view and single data input within a front-end 'wrap', instead of into many different systems.
- Reducing fraud and losses. Tighter tracking of activities, in-built cascading reviews and authority levels result in 'always on' audit and automatic audit trails.
- Faster time to market. Campaign planning systems allow templating succesful approaches and redoing best programmes with simple parameter changes, instead of redesigning / redoing them. Best practices in local sales / marketing activities can be transferred from one branch to another much faster.
- Improved skill base. Faster time to market and more campaigns with automated planning mean more knowledge gained in a given time-frame, giving better designed activities, sooner.
- Saving on direct marketing costs and reducing customer irritation. This can be achieved by cutting direct mail volume by fine-tuning revenue / expense-based targeting based on better propensity modelling, automating contact rules, co-ordinating branch level and central activities better and cutting repetitive, low return direct contacts.

Overall, a properly implemented CRM approach should result in the following quantifiable benefits:

- At least a 10% increase in new volumes booked;
- At least 2% incremental volume retained. (Note: this is not 2% increase in retention, this is an extra 2% portfolio staying with the bank; based on existing retention rates it can be anywhere from 2% upwards, when expressed as 'percentage increase in retention'.)

However, it should be noted that it normally takes about three years from implementation to realise these gains. In fact, some efficiency drops may occur during the first six months after implementation, as sales staff and others go through a learning process.

Alignments needed

Proper alignments and prerequisites should be in place to realise the benefits. Alignments and prerequisites are normally needed in three key areas:

1. Strategic:
    - A proactive business development model is needed, based on data insight, to take advantage of what CRM can offer.

2. Organisational:

   - Database marketing and sales process functions need to be in place to proactively manage getting benefits from CRM;
   - Extra support may be needed in departments such as Credit Risk Management and Operations to manage the increased volume in applications, bookings and portfolios;
   - A multi-channel approach is required for best results, either already integrated or ready to be integrated via CRM processes and systems.

3. Processes:

   - To automate the right processes, they need to exist first – if there are no acquisition or retention processes in place, they cannot be improved and automated through any CRM.

Architecture

Once alignments are in place, processes are optimised, benefit expectations defined the physical architecture implementation can start. Key pieces of a CRM architecture are, in order of priority and implementation:

1. Marketing data mart;
2. Contact management / sales force automation (SFA);
3. Marketing planning.

It is my firm belief that CRM must be a business-driven (as opposed to technology-driven) project. Therefore, it is up to the Sales area, together with Marketing, to drive the business requirement definition for CRM – what is it that Sales and Marketing need from the set-up to boost efficiencies? This can be an involved exercise. As a guide to this area, a short business requirements review is provided in Appendix B at the end of this chapter.

CRM is a very powerful approach to boost sales efficiencies when designed and implemented properly. However, it is easy to mis-design, mis-implement and mis-sell to staff.

Case study 9: How things can go wrong with CRM implementation

A very large retail banking subsidiary of a global bank learned this the hard way. Following the implementation of a contact management / SFA system, sales efficiencies decreased and results declined for five years before they could be fixed. When I reviewed what had happened, it was found that:

1. Front line sales staff 'relaxed' once the system was put in place, fully expecting that it would do at least part of their job, so results would come without hard work. By not using the tool in a disciplined way, the results of course did not materialise.
2. Sales management was reluctant to intervene because it felt 'intimidated' by the tracking capabilities of the new system. Without it being explained properly, the managers believed the system was actually implemented as a hidden audit tool to keep a closer eye on them. Therefore they neither dared to criticise it nor wanted to use it.
3. The corresponding marketing planning system was not implemented. Marketing therefore had great problems inputting data into the contact management system – it was very complicated, without the proper, fully integrated tool they needed. As a result, campaign planning was poor and use of the new system sporadic at best.
4. Top management believed that by implementing only part of a complex CRM set-up, the complexity level would be kept low and a close eye would not need to be kept on the project, which quickly became a technology initiative and resulted in all of the previously mentioned issues. But by the time problems were evident new technology projects were at the top of the priority list, needing management attention. So the 'old' CRM project got little management interest.

The issues were realised later and a proper CRM approach was designed, in an integrated way, driven by proper business leadership, supported by clear communication and strong training. Results improved – but a lot of opportunities had already been missed while struggling for years with a badly executed CRM approach. Hopefully this case study can serve as a checklist of watch-outs for the reader.

Service quality – controlling your channels

SQ, as can be seen by its many variations (Total Quality Management, Six Sigma, Quality Enterprise, etc) is a huge topic. As such, it goes well beyond the scope of this book. However, we must look at one specific aspect of it: how to set benchmarks and how to measure them across different channels. We must be careful, in an integrated multi-channel environment, to differentiate each channel, yet make sure they deliver the same high level of service, according to their different constraints.

It makes sense to break the large topic of 'service quality expectations' into four core areas:

1. Basic deliverables – key customer expectations regardless of channel;
2. SQ dimensions – the specific areas in which customers judge how the basics are delivered;
3. Measurement methods – tools used for measuring deliverables along the dimensions;
4. Service standards – our expectations, benchmarks.

Of these, 'basic deliverables' stay fairly constant across channels. They depend on the consumer, their basic needs and expectations, not on the bank. 'SQ dimensions' show some variability. For example, based on the channel being 'physical' or 'virtual', one may or may not have display materials which need to be clear and tidy to meet expectations. 'Measurement methods' may also change, based on the channel. Website access is hard statistical information, measured electronically. It is difficult to find an equivalent for a sales agent. Finally, 'service standards' show the greatest variability, reflecting not only channel differences, but environmental (e.g. time of day) and segment (e.g. VIP or core) ones as well.

The best way to make this come alive is to illustrate with real examples. Appendices C and D provide an outline of specific SQ definitions and measures for branches (as the standard) and call centres.

Appendix A M&A evaluation guidelines summary – a sales / marketing perspective

Reason

- Need consistent valuation of 'non-balance sheet items', to drive decisions from a sales efficiency perspective.

Components to review

- Customer base;
- Prospect base;
- Intermediary contacts;
- Channels;
- Brand strength;
- Marketing infrastructure;
- Personnel.

Values to be assigned

Customer base:

- 65% of acquisition costs (AC).

Prospect base:

- Ex-direct customer – 50% of AC;
- Ex-indirect customer – 15% of AC;
- Affiliates' customer – 15–25% of AC (depending on branding);
- Other lists – 5–15% of AC (depending on history).

Intermediary contacts:

- Retailer (loans) – 500% of AC;
- Agent (property) – 300% of AC;
- Lawyer (referrals) – 1,000% of AC;
- Sales agents – contract value.

Personnel:

- Six months' compensation.

Appendix B CRM architecture – summary of basic business requirements

Marketing data mart

- Ability to hold both customer and prospect databases, with relationship view at an individual level, plus householding capability (rolling up information to have a household level view);
- Deduplication facility to be able to check prospect and customer databases against each other, to avoid targeting customers for prospecting;
- Easy use with data mining analytical tools;
- Fast updates capability, at variable intervals (e.g. contact information daily, profit information quarterly);
- Ability to hold demographic, contact, profit (or proxy), behavioural information;
- Flexible fields for both internally and externally obtained information (e.g. sales cue, credit score, geo-code);
- Institutional memory: contact information, tracking customer response to previous offers, ability to pre-plan (diarise) follow-up activities;
- Link to all customer contact points.

Contact management / sales force automation

- Ability to capture and allocate sales leads;
- Link to data mart, with two-way updates (e.g. sales leads obtained from data mart, contact information fed back to data mart);
- Link to all customer contact points – all contact staff can see the same information about the customer, including full relationship view (all products and services), institutional memory (history of offers and responses to them), customer value;
- Link to operating system, one-way update (e.g. account is opened in the core system online, but account opened status fed back to contact management system overnight);
- Provide 'shell' screen for other systems (single log-on within a security shell, single information entry);
- Referral pass-over and follow-up capability;
- Leading indicator tracking (workload management, 'sales funnel');
- Cascading, variable access (e.g. branch manager vs. sales person, branch vs. branch, branches vs. branch agents, sales staff vs. sales agents, etc);
- Sales help modules (e.g. investor profiler, form printing, e-signature, product literature, sales scripts, etc).

Marketing planning

- Ability to automate data analysis to be done at predefined times in future: pre-programme events;
- Allow sequential campaign planning based on results of the previous one(s) – follow-up campaigns can be triggered automatically, information for action sent to Direct Marketing, call centre, Sales;
- Variable campaign planning based on both defined and undefined data;
- Plan direct marketing events, highlight conflicting actions;
- 'What if' capability, on-screen campaign planning;
- Automatic tracking, monitoring and reporting;
- Link to data mart and contact management systems.

Appendix C Service standards definition and measurement – sample outline for branches

Basic deliverables

These are usually the three main general expectations of an average retail customer when dealing with banks. They form the pillars of SQ-based approach.

- Efficiency:
  - Quick, accurate and consistent processing of all requests;
- Advice:
  - Professional and proactive advice, appropriate for the customer / prospect (not too high level, not too low level) which is easy to understand;
- Friendliness:
  - Helpful, respectful, competent, personalised service.

SQ dimensions

These are the areas of expectation where customers judge how the bank delivers on the three pillar requirements of high service quality.

- Accessibility:
  - Time spent waiting for service;
- Delivery speed:
  - Time needed to execute requests;
- Sales and service:
  - Adherence to prescribed sales and service procedures;
- Customer care:
  - Level of friendliness and empathy in customer interactions;
- Professionalism:
  - As in interactions with customers, being able to handle requests or calling on others to solve;
- Transparency:
  - Information and sales support materials displayed and used well;
- Branch appearance:
  - Cleanliness, orderliness, how inviting are exterior and interior.

Methods of measurement

These are some of the tools to assess quantitatively how well different channels and sales / service individuals deliver on the above SQ dimensions.

- Consumer research:
  - Conducted among own customers and competitors' customers, benchmarking the bank against main competitors in key SQ areas, establishing trend lines and goals;
- Mystery shoppers and mystery callers:
  - Conducted by trained professionals, unknown to the branch. They play the role of a customer / prospect and record their observations along the key dimensions listed;
- Internal observations:
  - Conducted by bank employees, external to the branch. Unlike mystery shoppers, their presence is known to branch staff. They observe staff interaction with prospects and customers and make suggestions for improvements;
- Self-assessment:
  - Performed by branch staff, using a standard checklist covering key areas of SQ dimensions;
- Complaint tracking:
  - Monitoring customer complaints and their resolution by branch, from a central source (usually Help Desk);
- SLA (service level agreement) tracking:
  - Tracking how well the branch delivered on its SLAs with other areas of the bank. This can be a useful diagnostic tool to identify problem areas before they become a customer service issue;
- Statistics:
  - Tracking sales efficiency indicators by the branch manager (conversion ratios, time spent in sales sessions, etc) can provide useful guidance.

Note that personal observations by the branch manager should be expected but should not normally be part of the formal service quality tracking and measurement systems. This is to ensure objective measuring and comparability across channels and outlets.

Service standards (benchmarks, expectations)

These are some of the specifics that can be measured under each of the dimensions to test for level of service delivery. The measurement tools to be used vary and will likely overlap in some areas.

Accessibility:

- Not more than three minutes waiting for quick transactions;
- Not more than five minutes waiting for sales consultation;
- Not more than 15 seconds to answer phone.

Delivery speed:

- Not more than one minute on hold if calling branch;
- Not more than one transfer of customer on phone line;
- Not more than 20 minutes to open new customer relationship (account for new customer);
- Not more than 10 minutes to open new account for existing customer;
- Not more than five minutes to initiate new feature / access mechanism to existing accounts (e.g. phone banking, internet, debit card);
- Not more than three minutes to initiate funds transfer, unless it involves currency exchange (in which case standard is 'not more than five minutes').

Sales and service:

- Proactively meet / greet customer;
- Tone is warm, personal, friendly;
- Direct requests are dealt with promptly;
- Appropriate questions are asked to understand customer's needs;
- Needs are summarised, confirmed;
- Adequate product knowledge is evident;
- Appropriate solutions to customer needs are offered;
- Product features are explained, their benefits matched to customer's needs;
- Sales support materials used during session (leaflets, brochures, summaries);
- Customer's acceptancc of solution offered is confirmed;
- Closure is attempted;
- Follow-up phone call or meeting is arranged (attempted) if closure is not successful;
- Alternative channels and access mechanisms suggested as appropriate – phone and internet banking, access cards, etc;
- Session is ended in a warm and friendly way;
- If sales session was held away from main traffic area (in separate office or designated area), accompany customer to exit or back to main branch area as appropriate.

Customer care:

- Staff smile and make eye contact with customers;

- Each sales individual is ready to take responsibility for solving the customer's problem;
- Customer concerns are either resolved or are taken over by one of the staff for follow-up;
- Follow-up steps planned and expected follow-up timetable (including expected timing for concern resolution) is communicated to the customer;
- Customer is treated with empathy, friendliness and professionalism.

Professionalism:

- Customer information is not left on desk, counter or computer screen when employee or customer are not present;
- Appropriate tone and (voice) volume is used with customers;
- Complex or confidential requests and emotional or upset customers are taken to a discrete area to deal with appropriately;
- Employees do not talk about customers or other staff members in the customer area of the branch or outside the branch;
- No private conversations among staff members in the customer area;
- No private phone calls taken by staff in the customer area;
- No eating, gum chewing or other inappropriate behaviour by staff in the customer area.

Transparency:

- Branch opening hours and bank contact details (call centre phone number, website address) posted on the door;
- Current terms, interest rates, exchange rates and other essential information are displayed visibly in the branch;
- Promotional posters in both the windows and inside are current;
- Brochure racks are well stocked with current materials;
- No misleading information on display anywhere;
- 24-hour self-service zone contains all essential materials – information, forms, etc.

Branch appearance:

- Branch exterior is clean (windows, doors, pavement area);
- Self-service area is clean and well-lit;
- Branch can be looked into from the outside;
- Lights are working, after hours as well;
- Counters and desks are tidy, no litter in branch or self-service area;
- Staff personal items kept out of view of customers.

Appendix D Service standards definition and measurement – sample outline for call centres

Note: The following guidelines are only for calls handled in person by call centre staff. Automated call response and interactive voice response (IVR) modules should be treated differently and tested statistically – both technically and with live test calls.

Basic deliverables

These are the same as for the branches (see Appendix C).

SQ dimensions

These are the same as for branches, except that 'Transparency' and 'Branch appearance' are omitted because they refer to physical outlets only.

Methods of measurement

These are the same as for the branches, but 'Statistics' take on a much greater role.

Service standards (benchmarks, expectations)

These should be adapted for the call centre environment.

Accessibility:

- Minimum 85% service level;
- Speed to answer not more than 20 seconds;
- Abandon rate not higher than 5%.

Delivery speed:

- Customer is not put on hold more than once in any given sales or service session block;
- Information delivery standard (average call time) to be set by the bank, based on its internal and external situation (e.g. strategic role of call centre, other channel availability, customer base composition, etc);
- Service delivery standard (average time to initiate order execution) also to be set by the bank, based on the same considerations as above.

Sales and service:

- Customer greeting is along standard lines, as defined in call centre training manual;
- Tone is warm, personal, friendly;

- Direct requests are dealt with promptly;
- Appropriate questions are asked to understand customer's needs;
- Needs are summarised, confirmed;
- Adequate product knowledge is evident;
- Appropriate solutions to customer needs are offered;
- Product features are explained, their benefits matched to customer's needs;
- Customer's acceptance of solution offered is confirmed;
- Closure is attempted;
- Referral to other channels (sales agent, branch, financial adviser, other) is initiated if customer does not want to close on the phone but is inclined to buy;
- Follow-up phone call or meeting is arranged (attempted) if needed, if closure is not successful and referral is not an option;
- Alternative channels and access mechanisms suggested as appropriate – internet banking, mobile phone banking, access cards, etc;
- Session is ended in a warm and friendly way.

Customer care:

- Each call centre representative is ready to take responsibility for solving the customer's problem;
- Customer concerns are either resolved or are taken over personally by the representative who received the call for follow-up;
- Follow-up steps planned and expected follow-up timetable (including expected timing for concern resolution) is communicated to the customer;
- Customer is treated with empathy, friendliness and professionalism;
- Customer contact rules are followed strictly when proactively calling – who can be called, about what, at what times, how many times in a given time-frame.

Professionalism:

- Policies and procedures governing in-bound and out-bound calls are followed;
- Employee is using appropriate tone and speed when speaking;
- No use of jargon, acronyms or internal bank lingo;
- No eating, drinking or gum-chewing when on call;
- Customer is not put on 'mute';
- No noise in the background (radio, personal phone, keyboard sound – other than when computer access is needed to deal with the customer);
- Standard phrases used for greeting, putting on hold, transferring, ending call.

www.ingramcontent.com/pod-product-compliance
Ingram Content Group UK Ltd.
Pitfield, Milton Keynes, MK11 3LW, UK
UKHW052302280926
15471UKWH00006B/1056

9 781907 720116